A DIVINE REVELATION OF SATAN'S DECEPTIONS

MARY K. BAXTER

A DIVINE REVELATION OF SATAN'S DECEPTIONS

WHITAKER
HOUSE

A DIVINE REVELATION OF SATAN'S DECEPTIONS

Mary K. Baxter
marykbaxter1@yahoo.com
www.marykbaxterinc.com

ISBN: 978-1-62911-331-9
eBook ISBN: 978-1-62911-332-6
Printed in the United States of America
© 2015 by Mary K. Baxter

Whitaker House
1030 Hunt Valley Circle
New Kensington, PA 15068
www.whitakerhouse.com

Library of Congress Cataloging-in-Publication Data

Baxter, Mary K.
  A divine revelation of Satan's deceptions / Mary K. Baxter.
    pages cm
  Includes bibliographical references
    ISBN 978-1-62911-331-9 (trade pbk. : alk. paper) — ISBN 978-1-62911-332-6
  (ebook : alk. paper) 1. Devil. 2. Spiritual warfare. 3. Private revelations. I. Title.
  BT982.B39 2015
  236'.47—dc23
                          2015015330

2 3 4 5 6 7 8 9 10 11 12 **ᴜᴜ** 23 22 21 20 19 18 17 16

Contents

Prologue:
Keys to the Kingdom

Upon this rock I will build my church; and the gates of hell
shall not prevail against it. And I will give unto thee the
keys of the kingdom of heaven: and whatsoever thou shalt
bind on earth shall be bound in heaven: and whatsoever
thou shalt loose on earth shall be loosed in heaven.
—Matthew 16:18–19 (KJV)

Jesus said, "Look, listen, and learn. I've given you the keys
to the kingdom. I want you to take a key in your hand in
the spirit." All at once, I looked at my hand, and there was
a spiritual key in it. "What do I do with it, Jesus?" I asked.
He said, "Come with Me." Then we were standing in front of
one of the large, transparent, glass-like cages. Something that
looked like a white glow was moving in it. I said, "What is this,
Lord?" He replied, "Take the key and put it in the lock and, in
My name, Jesus Christ, Emmanuel, Yeshua, open that door."

So I took the key. In the name of Jesus Christ, Emmanuel,
Yeshua, I put the spiritual key in the lock and turned it. The

lock broke open, and out flowed the most beautiful presence. Jesus had dropped to His knees, and He said, "My Spirit will once again flow over the earth and bring the people on the earth to conviction. My Spirit will again begin to draw people unto Me, child, by the thousands."

Introduction:
A Revelation for Today

As I have related in my previous books, Jesus Christ appeared to me in human form in 1976. I was an ordinary mother and homemaker, with a houseful of little children, who loved God with all her heart. Prophets and apostles had told me my calling, saying, "God's going to visit you and show you strange things that will shake the world." And God has fulfilled, and is fulfilling, that word.

When Jesus appeared to me, I had not died, and I was not dreaming; I was fully alert. By His power, for thirty nights, three hours a night, Jesus took me in spirit form into hell so that I could see its reality firsthand and warn people of the consequences of rejecting God the Father and His offer of forgiveness through His Son Jesus Christ. God is holy, and human beings were created in His image to be holy, also. But ever since the first man and woman turned their backs on God and disobeyed Him, people have been born with a sinful nature. To be restored to God, we must be cleansed by the blood of Jesus, who came to earth as a baby and grew into a man to die on the cross for us. He became our Substitute, receiving the punishment we deserved, and then He was gloriously resurrected from the dead by God the Father. Our part is to believe in Him, to repent of our sins, and to receive His sacrifice on our behalf so that we can be forgiven of all our wrongdoing and live a new life in Him.

Since the time when God first gave me revelations of hell, followed by ten days of revelations of heaven, I have spent my life ministering around the world, warning people of the reality of heaven and hell and telling them of God's extraordinary power to save us and equip us to do what He has called us to do. But God has recently taken me back to those first revelations. In 1976, when the journey of the thirty nights in hell was concluded, Jesus said to me, "I will close up your mind, and you will not remember some of the things I have shown and told you. But I will reopen your mind and bring back your understanding in the latter days. Then I will open up your remembrance and reveal to you the things I want put on paper. You will write a new book about hell. And I will raise up others who have seen hell and others who know about hell, and they will be witnesses to what I have shown you. For this purpose you were born, to write and to tell the things I show and tell you. There is much the world needs to know, for there is a beginning and an end to everything."

Jesus has brought many of those experiences back to my memory, and this book contains scenes from hell that I have not related in my other books. He opened up my mind and began to show me and tell me these things so that the world could know them now. These things are not pretty. I'm so glad Jesus Christ didn't allow me to remember everything at that time, because I couldn't have handled it then.

This revelation is for the times in which we now live. Through this book, I must tell these things that Christ has brought back to my remembrance for the world to understand.

In addition, a movie will be made that includes some of these experiences. I want it to be an excellent film that will clearly show the truth about hell. The Lord Jesus told me, "This is a book that will make the power of God shake this nation. You are a key, a key in the midst of a great revival I am going to bring." My response was and is, "Glory to Your name, Father. Spirit of the living God, have Your way."

We human beings have a dangerous adversary named Satan, or the devil. But we have a much more powerful God who is able to save and deliver us from any of his deceptions and attacks! Satan was once an archangel of God, but he wanted to usurp heaven's throne, and so he seduced a third of God's angels to rebel against Him. Satan and his angels were expelled from heaven. Yet the devil still seeks to seduce human beings, who are God's highest and most beloved creation. He wants us to rebel against our Creator so that we will fall further and further away from Him and ultimately be judged and sent to hell. Hell was prepared for the devil and his fallen angels; it was not intended for human beings. But it has become the destination of all who reject God.

Our God wants us to know that, in His power, we can stand against Satan's traps! *A Divine Revelation of Satan's Deceptions* is a call to recognize Satan's devices that keep people separated from God, prevent them from receiving Christ, and destroy them in hell. It contains revelation of how Satan has stolen and held captive the blessings that God has given to His people to accomplish His work in the world—blessings of anointing, gifts, resources, and more, which we must reclaim in these latter times. To do this, we need to obey God, renew our love for Him, and use specific "keys to the kingdom" that He has given us. God has called us to this so we can minister salvation, deliverance, and healing to the millions in the world who are dying and facing eternal judgment. These keys are described in the pages that follow.

We cannot allow Satan to deceive and rob us any longer. The Lord told me that this is a time for the judgment of demons. Satan and his forces of darkness can be defeated. We must fight back and reclaim our spiritual inheritance in the power of God.

My heart is full of new revelations that God has given me to tell the church. My heart is full of things that God has shown me, told me, and "downloaded" into me for many years. My heart is full of a desire to talk about the things that Jesus has revealed to me. There are truths of revelation that we need to understand. God said, *"My people are destroyed for lack of knowledge"* (Hosea 4:6). Therefore, I have tried my best to relate to you through this book some things that Christ first showed to me many years ago but has now revealed to the world. Jesus' words are not necessarily verbatim but do convey the messages that He gave to me.

God has given each believer a spiritual gift or gifts in order to build up the body of Christ. We all need one another if we are to grow more Christlike and be equipped to minister in His name to each other and to the world. Revelation and prophecy are the particular spiritual gifts that God has given me.

I have dedicated my life to communicating God's revelations. With His help, I will continue to do so for you and your family, for myself and my family, and for all the people of the world. We must come to a realization of the truth. The scales need to come off our eyes, and our ears need to be unstopped, so that we can see and hear what God is saying to us today. As I now relate some of the graphic details of hell, as well as the spiritual authority God has given us, get ready for a ride in the Spirit, for you'll never be the same.

Part 1:

Recognizing Satan's Deceptions

1

The Reality of Hell

When Jesus Christ took me into hell, I was in my spirit form, while my body remained on the earth. Jesus, however, was in human form. He looked about six feet four inches tall, and He was wearing a long white robe with a golden belt and sandals. His hair flowed to His shoulders, and He had a trimmed beard and mustache. He had beautiful blue eyes, and looking into those eyes was like looking into eternity. Everything about Him was so holy, pure, and precious. He was full of glory and of the fruit of the Spirit. (See Galatians 5:22–23.)

The Depths of an Eternity Without God

I looked down at Jesus' feet and saw large nail holes, and real blood seemed to be flowing from them. He took my hand, and my hand felt warm, even though I was in the spirit form. Blood from the nail hole in Christ's hand filled my hand and dripped to the ground. I screamed and said, "Oh, Jesus, why is this happening to You?" I looked at Him and saw big tears coming down His face. He said, "Child, for all these souls I died and shed My blood, but it is too late for them. But in this book you are doing—and it will be made into a movie—people shall see and know and understand the depths of eternity and of being lost without Me. The world needs to know this truth of an eternity without God. People need to understand the suffering and the pain that thousands and thousands are going through, while they go about life upon the earth, even as I call them to repent. This is a warning to the world to repent and to come back to the Lord Jesus Christ."

Repent therefore and be converted, that your sins may be blotted out, so that times of refreshing may come from the presence of the Lord.   **(Acts 3:19)**

"If I Had Only Known"

While Jesus and I were walking together in hell, it was a time of sorrow, of such sadness and grief, as I saw the millions of suffering souls. They looked like skeletons, and some of them were missing arms, legs, or other body parts. All of them had what looked like a dirty mist inside their ribcage—this was their eternal soul.

I looked around me as Jesus and I walked up a hillside. We were on a dusty, rocky, dirty road. Along the way, demons would run from Jesus, because He caused light to shine. They would scream, "What do we have to do with You?"[1] And then they would run away.

---

1. See Matthew 8:29; Mark 1:24; Luke 4:34.

We walked for a long time, and I smelled odors and saw flames in many areas. There were dark shadows in the mountains and caves. I heard souls screaming, "Let us out; let us out! Is there no more hope? There's no life down here, but yet I cannot die. Help me; help me!"

Around the top of the mountain, I saw high flames. Down below, in a valley full of dead men's bones, there was an army of thousands of skeletons, burning and screaming, "Let us die; let us die." As we walked past them, I could hear a multitude of voices crying such things as this: "Why didn't someone warn me? Why didn't someone tell me about this horrible place? I would have chosen the Lord and not lived such a wicked life, if I had only known." I looked at Christ as tears came down His face, and I had pity and great compassion for Jesus.

The ground was all smoky and black, and there was an evil-looking darkness everywhere. But Jesus caused a light to shine, and the darkness went away for a while. He sat down on a big rock that overlooked a valley of high flames, and I sat by Him, very scared. We were far up on a mountainside, and I was so tired from hearing all those cries of regret, all that grief and sorrow.

As we sat, I looked over into the valley. About half a mile down, there was a greenish-yellow mist hanging over some fires. Christ was crying. I kept looking at His feet and wanting to wipe the blood away. I thought, *Thousands and thousands are here, and more are coming. What can I do, Lord? What can I do?* He put His arm around me and pulled me close to His side.

Then Jesus looked at me and, calling me by my middle name, said, "Katherine, you see all of this?" He waved His hand, and as He did, the fog and mist moved back, and I could see thousands of skeletons burning and screaming, "Let us die; let us die. We cannot die. We cry for death, and death doesn't come." I looked at them and said, "Jesus, please get them out. Please give them flesh and bone and make them new again, Lord." But Jesus said, "It's too late. This is the judgment of My Father upon the sins of the flesh. I was manifested to destroy the works of Satan[2] so people would know and understand how he deceives. People are doing the wicked things of the world—cursing, lying, cheating, hating, refusing to forgive; committing adultery and fornication; practicing witchcraft and sorcery. Satan deceives people, child. God has rules and laws and regulations concerning these things, and the key is to repent. Tell the people to repent and to ask Me to forgive them, come into their heart, and save their soul, and I will."

If you confess with your mouth the Lord Jesus and believe in your heart that God has raised Him from the dead, you will be saved. For with the heart one believes unto righteousness, and with the mouth confession is made unto salvation. **(Romans 10:9–10)**

I looked at Jesus' face, so stern and so sad, and I put my arm around Him and fell onto His chest, crying; yet no tears came from me, because I was in the spirit form. I remember thinking about my home—my children and other family members. I looked at the Lord and said, "Jesus, what can I

---

2. See 1 John 3:8.

do? I am a mother, and I have children. I never want my children to come here, Jesus. Promise me they won't." I looked up at His eyes, and He said, "Child, ahead of you is greater horror and great sorrow, but I will give you the strength to go through this. I will give you the anointing to go through this, and it will help thousands come unto Me."

Jesus spoke to me with deep compassion and great love, saying, "Child, I'm walking you through hell to show you the depths, degrees, and levels of torments. I'm showing you the truth. My leaders on the earth are lying to people. Yes, many are telling the truth, but many others tell people that there is no hell and that they can live in whatever way they want. They say that God is good and therefore would never send anyone to an eternal punishment. But My Father is a righteous Judge. My Father is a holy Judge. In the Holy Bible, it tells you not to commit the sins of the flesh once you come to the knowledge of repentance and truth.[3] My Word will stand forever. Child, it's too late for all of these, but I want you to hear them."

Awake, and Seek the Lord

I looked down at the Lord's feet and again saw the nail holes with the blood flowing out. I began to think about the Holy Scriptures, which describe how Jesus was beaten for me and for all other people so we wouldn't have to go to hell, if we would only believe that He is the Son of God, that He came to earth and died on the cross to save us from eternal damnation, and that His blood will wash us clean as we repent of our sins and begin to live for God.

I looked again where all the flames were coming from, very high at the end of the massive army of skeletons that

3. See Hebrews 10:26.

were burning and screaming and gnashing their teeth. Every so often, I would see something like corrupt flesh grow on the skeletons' bones, and then the flames would burn it off, and the bones would be dry, and worms would crawl out of them. I thought about the masses of people in the world who need the Lord—now, in this very hour.

I saw demons who had eyes of red fire and skin that was like black coal. They had horns on their heads, with fire coming out of them. They had wings full of maggots. And they had an odor that was beyond belief. It smelled like rotten flesh, like sewers and dung, like burning oil.

We resumed walking, and I saw that as Christ walked, He left blood on the ground. I screamed, "Jesus, where are we going?" He said, "I am going to show you this, and then you will return home. Then again, tomorrow night, we will come back to the same place." I said, "Jesus, I don't know if I can do this." He answered, "I will give you the strength and the courage to do this." I clung tightly to Jesus' hand and noticed that there was no blood there now. I looked at His feet, and they, too, were dry. We continued walking, and I kept crying, although no tears came. My heart was breaking, and I was thinking about the earth. *There is so much manipulation and so much sin and so much evil and so much death. Will the world listen to me? Will people understand that there is an eternity without God for those who do evil and reject Him? The world has many theories and many lies; and so many preachers are telling people one thing or another that is not true. Awake, awake, men and women of God; seek the Lord while He can be found.*

Seek the Lord while He may be found, call upon Him while He is near. Let the wicked

forsake his way, and the unrighteous man his thoughts; let him return to the LORD, and He will have mercy on him; and to our God, for He will abundantly pardon.

(Isaiah 55:6–7)

There Is Hope in Jesus

I then began to think of the love of God and of hope in Jesus Christ. From the mountaintop, I turned around and looked right into the eyes of the Lord, and He said to me, "There is hope in Me. There is deliverance in Me. Warn the people to return unto Me; tell them that once again I want to raise up the fivefold ministry[4] where the people need hope. They need to know that I am their Anchor, and that they can put their trust and their hope in Me, the Lord Jesus Christ."

We are in the midst of a precarious world situation today, as you well know. But if you turn to the Lord Jesus Christ, there is hope. He wants us to look to Him. He wants to heal us. He wants to stop the evil. He wants to stop the wars. He wants us to live with Him forever. There is hope for us and for our families and for the generation of our children and grandchildren. There is hope in Jesus Christ. Turn to Him with all your heart, all your mind, all your soul, and all your strength. (See Matthew 22:37; Luke 10:27.) Jesus will make you an overcomer.

Blessed be the God and Father of our Lord Jesus Christ, who according to His abundant

4. See Ephesians 4:11–12.

mercy has begotten us again to a living hope through the resurrection of Jesus Christ from the dead, to an inheritance incorruptible and undefiled and that does not fade away, reserved in heaven for you, who are kept by the power of God through faith for salvation ready to be revealed in the last time.

(1 Peter 1:3–5)

Recognizing Satan's Deceptions:

Satan tries to deceive us into thinking that it will be a long time before we die, so we can put off receiving Jesus Christ and serving God. Don't be caught in that trap. If you don't know Jesus as your Savior, or if you have fallen away from God, you can be restored to Him right now by praying the following prayer and making a commitment to love and serve Him. Please say this prayer:

Heavenly Father,

I believe in You and in Your Son Jesus Christ, who came to earth to die on the cross for my sins. I believe that You raised Him from the dead and that He is alive forever, so that everyone who believes in Him can receive eternal life. Because of what Jesus did for me, I ask You to forgive all my sins and to come into my heart and save my soul. Fill me with Your Holy Spirit, and help me to live for You from this day forward. Thank You for saving me and giving me a new life. In Jesus' name, amen.

2

Multitudes of Every Nation

The next night, Jesus spoke, and I was again walking with Him in hell. He said, "Come on, child, I want to show you something in the jaws of hell. Hell has a body. Remember that in the middle of the earth there are degrees of fire, torment, and judgment of God. And at the great white throne judgment, when death and hell are brought up out of here to stand in the galaxies, those here will be judged out of the books that were written—which say that they never repented of their sins and that their sins were never washed in My blood—and they'll be thrown into the lake of fire, My daughter, because their names are not in the Book of Life."[5]

All at once, we went into another area, and I could feel the earth move under my feet. As we walked, Jesus said, "God made the soul of man and woman to live forever. This is the judgment of My Father on sin. Their judgment is set." Then He repeated, "They will be here till the great white throne judgment of God, and then they'll be put in the lake of fire." I felt so helpless. Jesus told me, "I am the way, the truth, and the life, Katherine."[6] I heard the cries of the dead get louder and louder, and I knew that they had been there for years—years

5. See Revelation 20:11–15.
6. See John 14:6.

23

of sorrow, years of grief, years of pain, years of weeping and gnashing of teeth, years of burning yet not burning up.

Jesus knew my thoughts, and He said, "Child, if a person is blind in one eye and then dies and comes to hell, he is blind in hell. If someone comes to hell who has had cancer, the cancer is ten times worse; the pain is that much worse. The flames come over them, the worms crawl through them, and they feel the excruciating fire of the eternal judgment of God. My Father sent Me so that people would not come here, child. But they have mocked Me on the earth; they've made fun of Me, child. They've said that I'm not real. They tell all kinds of lies about My holy Word. And God has a plan. He planned for you, My daughter—a mother, a housewife—to come and see all these horrible things, to write books and make records of what's in the middle of the earth. This is your mandate; this is your calling. And you will know and understand in the days ahead how much more I have for you."

During my time in hell, I learned that demons also give bottles of acid to those who were alcoholics on earth; when they drink it, the acid burns them, and they scream. Those who murdered people are stabbed by demons over and over again, but they cannot die. Those who raped little children have their bones torn apart by demons. (See Psalm 50:22.) World, wake up; wake up! Hell is your fate if you do not repent. (See Luke 12:40–48; Matthew 24.) May the Lord God have mercy on the world.

"They Would Not Listen"

We kept on walking. I wanted to run. I wanted to cry. I wanted to pull the people out of the fire and put flesh on them, but I couldn't do that. I had no power. It was horrible.

I thought, *I hope I don't see anybody I know,* because I knew many people who had died without Jesus. The dead were screaming, "Let us die. We know we've sinned against God. Oh, can you forgive us now, Jesus?"

The cries of the dead were getting worse and worse, and I screamed, "Oh, God, is there nothing You can do?" There were multitudes and multitudes of voices of every nation. The demons would come up and stab people with something and say, "Shut up! Satan is king here." And they would put more fire on the souls.

Some of the skeletons were in holes, some in caves, and some behind rocks. Others were in vats of fire, salted with fire, bobbing up and down. And on the vats was written "The abominations of desolations." I said, "Oh, God, what is that in the jaws of hell?" He said, "Child, they are those who used to preach My Word, but they lied. They mixed a perverse spirit with My Word and made it seem like I was a phony God. I've loved them, My daughter, but they would not listen. And they caused many to go to hell. You have seen them in our walk through hell. So, My Father judged them. The Father is a holy God, a righteous God, a sincere God. He knows all things, Katherine."

It is appointed for men to die once, but after this the judgment.   **(Hebrews 9:27)**

Death was all around, but no one dies in hell. They just keep burning and burning and burning. They cry and scream from unbearable pain. There is no relief; they cannot sleep, and they cannot pass out.

I knew about my heavenly Father's judgment on sin, and I looked down at Jesus' feet and saw the blood flowing. But I noticed that when He walked, the blood disappeared immediately. I thought about how many times on the earth I had pleaded His precious blood—the covenant of God—over me, my family, and other people for healing and protection. As I looked at Jesus, I said, "Lord, this is covenant; Jesus is our covenant. We have to bring the ark of the covenant [the Holy Word of God] back. Jesus is the One who was sent to deliver us from eternal damnation."

The Lord said, "Katherine, I'm going to raise up—and I have already risen up—many others who have seen hell, and it's going to be a witness to what I've shown you. And there shall be a day, My daughter, when this movie will be made, and I the Lord will put a great anointing upon it; I will make the people listen. For you and others have suffered greatly to write this, to tell this, if they'll just listen. For Satan does not want the people to listen to the truth. Satan wants the people to have 'fun' in evil ways, perverse ways, unclean ways. But My Father said, 'Be ye holy, for I am holy.'[7] And if the people do sin, tell them to repent. For they have an Advocate now through Me. I will travail to the Father for them. And I will forgive them if they will be real and call on Me, Katherine. I'm showing you all of this so that you and your family will be saved, and masses of others."

I thought of various family members, friends, and others who did not believe that God created the world with His word (see Psalm 33:6) and did not acknowledge everything He has done for us. Hell was made for the devil and his angels (see Matthew 25:41), but hell has enlarged itself to hold

---

7. See, for example, Leviticus 11:44–45.

lost souls—the souls of those who would not listen to God and repent (see Isaiah 5:14).

My little children, these things I write to you, so that you may not sin. And if anyone sins, we have an Advocate with the Father, Jesus Christ the righteous. And He Himself is the propitiation for our sins, and not for ours only but also for the whole world.

(1 John 2:1–2)

I thought, *Jesus, it hurts so bad to see a skeleton burning that used to have flesh and hair and organs, that was alive on the earth having a good time while the sun was shining and they were enjoying the fresh air and beautiful things. And to think they died in their sins, and when their soul came out of their body, demons brought them down here to give them the punishment related to the sin they committed the most during their lifetime.* When I looked at Jesus, He said, "Child, it's too late for all of these you see burning and screaming and weeping, because they would not listen. They wanted the world and the lusts thereof more than Me and the Father's commandments. I do not want you to fret or worry, because I have so much power, daughter; I have all power in heaven and earth and in between.[8] I'm giving you this testimony to tell the world so that people do not come here. If the world would repent of their sins and look to God, He would hear them.

---

8. See, for example, Matthew 28:18.

"Hell is a holding place till the great day of the great white throne judgment, when their books, which are all in hell, will be brought before the throne of God and opened. Their books were never washed in My blood. My people—those who love Me and try their best to keep the commandments of God—will not be judged, My daughter; they've been washed in My blood and cleansed and saved from eternal damnation. My commandment is 'Love you one another as I have loved you.'[9] Katherine, help Me to win the lost. Tell the people what is here. I will anoint the message with truth and the fear of the Lord. Also, I will keep those who turn to Me. If they would repent of their sins and ask Me to forgive them and come into their heart and save their soul, I would. I'm going to raise up many young people to preach the gospel."

There is therefore now no condemnation to those who are in Christ Jesus, who do not walk according to the flesh, but according to the Spirit. For the law of the Spirit of life in Christ Jesus has made me free from the law of sin and death. (Romans 8:1–2)

"My Father, Have Mercy"

Jesus said, "This place is so horrible and sad. This place is so hot and evil. This place is so demonic." Fire was burning. Snakes were crawling around. Rats weighing from one pound to seventy pounds were biting the souls. There was grief, fear,

---

9. See John 13:34; 15:12.

and sorrow. There was hatred in many places. The cries of the dead were everywhere. They were the cries of men and women of every nation. Some souls were blaspheming God, some were crying, and some were saying, "Is there no more hope?" These souls had the pleasures of sin for a season. Some had enjoyed hurting people. Now they were in hell.

We came to another rock and sat down. I was so exhausted, yet I was grateful that my family members were in their beds, asleep, and that God's angels were all around them, watching over them. I knew that almighty God would take care of me; He would watch over me and my family.

I had all my faculties—my thoughts and my emotions. I knew exactly what was going on; I knew exactly what I was seeing. I knew that this was Jesus Christ. I knew that I knew that almighty God was showing me this revelation to help everybody understand the reality of what is hidden and invisible. I began to get angry at the devil. As Jesus and I had walked in hell, I had seen the burned ground and the thousands and thousands of skeletons burning and screaming. I had seen the sections in hell where liars were kept; the sections where abusers of men and women were held; the sections for those who been in pornography; the sections for those who had practiced perverse sins and unclean sex acts, and whose souls were burning and screaming and running to try to put out the fires that were burning their bodies, but could not.

Every so often, Jesus would let me see real flesh grow on the skeletons. For a little while, they would look the same as human beings on earth, but then all at once their flesh would melt down like hot lava, and worms would teethe on their bones and cause them great pain. They would scream, "Help me. Doesn't anybody care for me? Why didn't somebody warn me?" And Jesus said, "Katherine, tell My people to read the Bible. Tell My people to listen to worship music. Tell My people to find good churches to go to."

I said, "Jesus," and then I sat on a rock. Jesus said, "Come and sit with Me." He had on the white robe and sandals, and the golden belt around His waist. Jesus put His hands on His face and began to pray, "My Father, My Father, have mercy, have mercy." As He began to pray and travail, hell shook. Words came out of Him from the depths of His soul. And I knew He understood that souls are eternal. So many liars on the earth will tell you that you don't have an eternal soul. You do. And I could hear Jesus screaming, and suddenly hell shook at the violence of it. The fires died down. Some of the souls who were in the pits fell over on the sides. For some of the skeletons, the pain stopped for a few minutes. And Jesus' face was covered with tears. His love is so strong. His acts were of love, and He grieved so over everything He was showing me.

He said, "Child, come sit." I was feeling so helpless, so afraid. I thought, *Oh, God, what if I had died when I was backslidden from You? What if that was me when I was in sin, Lord? What if You had not saved me? When I had my car wreck, I could have died. The doctors took my spleen out, and I was in the hospital for days. God, I could be here with the rest of them. I thank You for Your mercy. Thank You for Your grace.* I was so afraid.

Jesus said to me, "Peace, be still." I remembered that He had said the same words to many of the skeletons when He had talked with them, just as we will see in later chapters. He would go up to one of them and ask, "O man, what are you doing here? What is your name?" I remember the skeletons telling Him the things they had done on the earth, and that they did not want their family to come there. He'd say, "Peace, be still," and the demons would run away from Him and scream, "Don't say that word here!"

When Jesus told me, "Peace, be still," immediately, a peace came over me. And Jesus said, "I will direct your steps. These things you will write and you will tell. I will have you write books about hell and heaven, My daughter."

I became scared again. I'd been walking such a long way before we sat down. I was very tired, but I could not sleep. I was hungry, but I could not eat. I was thirsty, but there was no water. I was sad, but I could not cry. My only hope was in Jesus, being next to Him. And Jesus was so very close. He took my left hand and said, "I'm leading you, and woe be to those who hurt you or judge you, for I am the Lord who loves thee. You've given your life for Me. I want the world to know. And yes, you'll be mocked, you'll be laughed at, you'll be scoffed at, but that's okay. Satan is going to fall, his kingdom is going to fall. I took from him the keys of death and hell, daughter.[10] There are many mysteries to Satan; there are many things that haven't been told yet; there are yet many more revelations. But I say, 'Come on, little one, come on.'" He pulled me close to His side, and I felt such peace.

What If That Was You?

And then I heard the cries of the dead again, and they began to curse God in all things. I said, "Lord, this is horrible." I looked below, and a large circle of fire came up in the air. I thought, *All things were created by God.* He had

10. See Revelation 1:18.

created the souls of the people who were now in the flames down there burning and crying out to die but being unable to. Think about it. What if that was you? Imagine being thrown into hell so that you never slept again, never ate again, never got to pray again, never even got to do anything wicked again. You would simply be burning and burning and remembering.

Yes, the dead remember their life on earth. In Jesus' parable of the rich man and the beggar named Lazarus, the rich man was aware that he was in hell. That could be you or me, if it had not been for God's grace. He wants to save you. You do have an eternal soul. That's why I am pouring out my heart to you, so that you will listen and hear the truth about hell. Go to God and receive His offer of forgiveness in Jesus right now.

There was a certain rich man who was clothed in purple and fine linen and fared sumptuously every day. But there was a certain beggar named Lazarus, full of sores, who was laid at his gate, desiring to be fed with the crumbs which fell from the rich man's table. Moreover the dogs came and licked his sores. So it was that the beggar died, and was carried by the angels to Abraham's bosom. The rich man also died and was buried. And being in torments in Hades, he lifted up his eyes and saw Abraham afar off, and Lazarus in his bosom. Then he cried and said, "Father Abraham, have mercy on me, and send Lazarus that he may dip the tip of his finger in water and cool my tongue; for I am tormented in this flame." But Abraham said, "Son, remember that in your lifetime you received your good things, and likewise Lazarus evil things; but now he is comforted and you are tormented. And besides all this, between us and you there is a great gulf fixed, so that those who want to pass from here to you cannot, nor can those from there pass to us." Then he said, "I beg you therefore, father, that you would send him to my father's house, for I have five brothers, that he may testify to them, lest they also come to this place of torment." Abraham said to him, "They have Moses and the prophets; let them hear them." And he said, "No, father Abraham; but if one goes to them from the dead, they will repent." But he said to him, "If they do not hear Moses and the prophets, neither will they be persuaded though one rise from the dead." (Luke 16:19–31)

Recognizing Satan's Deceptions:

Satan tries to deceive us into thinking that God doesn't exist or that we don't need Him; we can just enjoy the pleasures of sin without worrying about the consequences. Don't fall into this trap. Romans 14:12 says, "So then each of us shall give account of himself to God." What account of your life could you give to God right now?

3

Hell Is Not Your Home

As I walked with Jesus along the pathway high in the mountains of hell, every so often, I would feel a hot wind blow. It seemed as if there were certain places in hell that were so cold and yet so hot. And winds would blow through and make the flames hotter.

The Responsibility of a Prophet

I was thinking about my life ahead, about my family and friends, and about eternity, and I thought, *Surely, Jesus Christ, the Son of God, has all power in heaven and on earth and everything in between. What Christ is showing me is a big responsibility.* Without a doubt, what my Father has commanded me to do has been a great responsibility. I was awakened to an immense reality when God sent His Son Jesus to actually translate me to the bowels of the earth to walk among the dead in hell. I had an obligation to record what I saw and to find a publisher and complete the book, so that the world could know that hell is real but that God has provided forgiveness for us through Jesus Christ.

As I was thinking about this responsibility, the Lord Jesus said to me, "Katherine." I answered, "Yes, Lord." He continued,

"I have brought forth many others in the last few years to confirm what I have shown you down here and in heaven. I will bring others yet, My daughter. As I see the Father do, I do."

I looked at the King, and He was wearing a crown and holding a scepter in one hand. He is my King, and I must obey Him. He never promised me it would be easy. When God calls you and chooses you for a mighty work, you truly pay a price. You often go through a lot in life to prepare for such a calling and to carry it out. And even though you do rely on your fellow believers for prayer and encouragement and other things, you must ultimately seek God's counsel and wisdom rather than man's.

And Jesus came and spoke to [His disciples], saying, "All authority has been given to Me in heaven and on earth. Go therefore and make disciples of all the nations, baptizing them in the name of the Father and of the Son and of the Holy Spirit, teaching them to observe all things that I have commanded you; and lo, I am with you always, even to the end of the age." Amen.
(Matthew 28:18–20)

The King of the Living

I opened up my mind, my heart, and my spirit to the Lord Jesus. I looked up again, and He was no longer wearing the crown or holding the scepter. He said to me, "Child, I do not want to be a King of the dead. I want to be a King of the living. You are going to bring life to many through this responsibility. And I give you a promise: For those who try to harm this work or to take it from you deliberately and willfully, the judgment of the Lord will be swift and quick upon them. Those who do it innocently will be judged differently. Now come; let's go. The covenant of God stands for you and your family, and I will bring them all unto Me, daughter, I promise you."

As we began to walk on this dark and ugly mountain of black soot and burned rocks, I heard growls that sounded as if they were coming from huge animals; I did not know what these sounds were. I held tightly to the Lord's hand, and strength came into me as I kept walking with the King.

Then, much light appeared around Jesus and me. The sirens of death were around me, too, the cries of men and women, some of them screaming, "Have mercy; let me die," and others blaspheming and screaming cries of regret, such as "Why didn't someone warn me?" Again, I felt such responsibility.

I heard a growl, and ahead of me was a large, ugly demon with a face like a lion and a body like a serpent, with clawed feet and a long tail full of fire. I saw that it had many arms, and then I noticed it also had other heads. I said, "Jesus, what in the world is that?" Jesus spoke to the demon and said, "You will remove yourself from this pathway, for I adjure you in the name of God Almighty." The demon fell down on the ground and withered into a small worm. Christ stepped on it, and fire and blood came out of His feet, destroying the demon. I looked at the Lord, and He looked at me and said, "I am your

King. I am able to destroy many things, for it is the time of the judgment of many demons to be destroyed in the earth and in the galaxies."

I said, "Lord, is that another mystery, another revelation?" He said, "Yes, My daughter, yes. In My holy name, the Lord Jesus Christ, Emmanuel, Yeshua, I will begin to release teaching and wisdom and knowledge on that revelation, for in My name, great things are done. Come."

He continued, "I never want you to have a divided heart—a heart that loves Me one day and a heart that doesn't love Me the next day. I know your heart. I made your heart. I have been with you through all those dilemmas. And now, let's look ahead." We kept walking, and the King no longer spoke. Everything became quiet, even the voices of the dead. We were so far away from them, I could barely hear them.

You shall love the Lord your God with all your heart, with all your soul, with all your mind, and with all your strength.
(Mark 12:30)

Satan's Throne

"What's ahead of me, Jesus?" I asked, and I pulled on His hand. He replied, "My child, Satan is very, very evil. His days are numbered. And this is a place where the blood of many whom he has killed falls down like a waterfall. Remember, he is a fallen angel. Remember, he knew many secrets of God. Remember, he understood about the blood covenant—that I gave My life for the world. I am going to show you evil things that he has done. I will give you the strength to see them, the strength to record them, the strength to tell about them. You will receive more wisdom and knowledge concerning the revelation of hell, and others will, too, child, through the new book you will write."

The King and I were standing at the top of a mountain of darkness. I looked into the darkness, and Jesus raised His hand; He was holding a scepter again. A flame shot out, and the darkness became light. He said, "Child, I am using a different scepter down here. This is the Scepter of Revelations. And now, as you are looking at this next scene, this will help to open the eyes of thousands of people as you tell about it or write it. My angels are with us."

Before me was a huge opening, larger than the Grand Canyon. What I saw in this opening was very clear and detailed. In different sections were many demonic beings and skeletons. There was also a wide, foul-smelling stream of flowing blood, at least a mile wide, which came off a high part of another mountain. It flowed down, and then it went into something like a cavern and finally to a river. Jesus told me that this stream was really an illusion manufactured by Satan to symbolize the death and destruction that he had inflicted upon the earth. There were times when the flow of blood was visible, and times when it would vanish. This cascade of blood was fed by at least three smaller falls/streams that flowed into it, each one related to the spiritual state in which people had died.

The Lord said, "This is the blood of many, My daughter, who have died without Me, as well as the blood of the innocent people Satan has killed." After seeing this stream of blood, I understood why I saw blood flowing in hell at times.

The Jesus said, "Look over there." I looked, and there was a room with gold walls, such as a king would have, which was wide open in the front; it seemed to be about half a mile long. There was also a gold ceiling with chandeliers. Everything looked so immaculate and beautiful.

And then I saw a throne—and there sat Satan! He was facing the blood that was flowing down. I can't really describe it as a waterfall, but it was full of blood, all blood. And Satan was laughing about it.

On either side of the throne was a large demon. One of the demons was standing next to the devil, holding a scroll. He was perhaps thirteen feet high and very round, with three heads, a hairy body, six arms, and about six legs. He looked as if he weighed two thousand pounds. Opening up the scroll, he held it to the devil's face, saying, "O King, we will win against God. The list has increased of those who have lost their souls."

The devil was very large, as well. He had a big face and huge horns; his countenance was like the face of a man, although part of his head was crushed. He had a wide chest, about four feet across, and huge, muscular arms. He also had very large, muscular legs. And he had webbed feet and claws. Sometimes his body appeared to be red, and sometimes it appeared to be brown.

As he sat there, he turned into a good-looking man wearing a suit. Satan stood up and said, "I know the secrets, because I was in heaven. I know what temptations to send a man through women and other lusts of the flesh to destroy him. I know that my voice has not yet been destroyed, but if my force of evil was ever shut down, I would not be able to seduce so many people. And I am letting all you demons hear this and know this."

I noticed that there was an opening at one part of the vision. But then Jesus corrected me, saying, "It is not a vision, My child; it is real." He knew my thoughts.

Almighty God Is Greater Than Satan

Standing in an area in this valley were what seemed like a million demons. Satan turned to them and said, "It is your job never to allow this revelation of my strength and my courage and my power to be revealed to the prophets or the apostles or the people; for there truly is a judgment on me, and I will be thrown in the lake of fire one day because God has said so. But I've taken the wisdom I learned in heaven and the wisdom I've learned of man as my own wisdom and knowledge, and I've seduced thousands and thousands into hell through the lust of their flesh, which they desired more than God's commands; and the bloodfall there is a result of my wisdom." I trembled and said, "Oh, God, how can this be?" Jesus looked at me and said, "Listen, child."

I watched and listened again as Satan sat back down on the throne and returned to his original appearance. He laughed and said, "I have the power to change my form anytime I want, and I have given that power to some of my demons that are going to be roaming the earth. I have many plans of evil. I will seduce many people so that they will not follow Jesus Christ."

We are in a war against Satan and his powers of darkness. We must seek God, pray, and take a strong stand against the devil on behalf of the lost.

For Satan himself transforms himself into an angel of light.   (2 Corinthians 11:14)

Another demon came over carrying a different scroll that said "The Deeds of Evil of Satan." I saw the writing. And I heard unspeakable things, earthshaking things. Jesus said to me, "What he speaks shall not be, for in My name, the name of the Lord Jesus Christ, I rebuke all these things he has spoken and has written, Katherine. The Father, the Holy Spirit, and I agree together that this shall not be.

"Now, My child," said Christ, "we will go to another part of hell, and you will see more unspeakable, horrible things that Satan does to souls. These souls used to preach My gospel, but Satan seduced them, tempted them to backslide, and caused them to die. I spared many such souls before they died, but I want My prophets, My apostles, My preachers, My evangelists, and My chosen to hear this. I have called them. Clean out your hearts, your minds, and your souls. Come forth to Me and tell Me the truth. I will understand. I will forgive you and wash you clean. Don't think you will have tomorrow, because sometimes tomorrow never comes." I just hung my head and thought of my own weaknesses. I remembered things that I have had to repent of, and I said to myself, *Oh, God, oh God, how can we—*

But Jesus didn't let me finish my thought. He said, "You will overcome by the blood of the Lamb and the word of your testimony; and I am able to make all My people overcome if they will listen to Me. Satan does not know everything. He thinks he does, but he does not. My Father is greater, and He has greater plans than Satan could ever think of. My Father could erase that knowledge from him in a second, My child. And eventually, He will do that. But man has a will, and at this point in time, God wants that will to be toward Him, and Satan wants that will to serve him. This is definitely a war, a spiritual war. But greater is almighty God. Remember, He created Satan. There are many mysteries and much knowledge you will never understand, and other people won't, either, because God doesn't want them to. But I say, 'Look up, look up, My child, and trust Me.'" And with that, we were leaving hell, and I was going back to my home.

And they overcame him by the blood of the Lamb and by the word of their testimony, and they did not love their lives to the death.
(Revelation 12:11)

Recognizing Satan's Deceptions:

In what ways does Satan appear as an "angel of light," making things that are evil appear to be good so that people will be ensnared by them? Is there anything in your own life that many people would say is acceptable but is actually contrary to God's Word or His plan for your life? Don't allow yourself to fall into this trap. Repent of any sin and be reconciled to God. You were saved by His grace, and He will welcome you back.

After you have been restored to God, make a commitment to no longer yield to the desires of the sinful nature, or the flesh. Learn to control those desires. Jesus said that we must deny ourselves, take up our cross, and follow Him. (See, for example, Mark 8:34.) If you find yourself yielding to those desires, repent immediately and maintain a close relationship with God.

4

Seducing Powers

Demonic Deception and Destruction

Jesus said, "Now we have to go to another place here in hell, child. And this is a place that is so horrifying. It's how Satan works on the earth to bring deception to the people through lust. There are seducing powers out there that pull people into great lust and perversion and demonic activity. Demon powers have also caused many people to commit suicide, and God has great mercy on these souls, Katherine.

"There are times and seasons when God's power moves on the earth. You're going to need My power, child. You're going to need My anointing. And many others are going to need it to bring back the ark of God [the holy Word of God, His covenant with us]. For Satan is running rampant in the earth, bringing forth much witchcraft, much occult on television and in the movies, much demonic activity, but My Word can counteract him and deliver people from his destructive grasp.

"And I'm telling you, little children are being raped, beaten, and murdered by demonic powers operating in people whom they have possessed. Little children who are innocent and pure. And My Father is grieved over this. There are absolutely no babies, no little children, in hell. My Father is merciful. He takes them to heaven when they die. He gives them new bodies, and there is great joy in heaven over them. They're taught; they go to school in heaven. Some of them grow up in heaven; some of them stay small until their mother and father come to heaven, and then they meet them at the gates of glory, and they grow up in heaven with them.

"My Father has so much in heaven—golden streets; body parts in storehouses, ready to be poured on the earth where Satan has mutilated people. God is getting ready to bring an avalanche of miracles to the earth. He sees the suffering of the saints. He sees that you're living in times like those in the book of Daniel, where many are so afflicted by the enemy, and He sees how the saints pray and travail, and how there seems to be no end to the sorrow. But the Lord has sent mighty angels to help you and many other saints to know Him and to obey Him, Katherine."

I said, "It's my greatest desire, Lord." Jesus wants us to heal the sick, raise the dead, and allow the Holy Spirit to draw people to God through us!

Are not all angels ministering spirits sent to serve those who will inherit salvation?
(Hebrews 1:14 NIV)

Demonic Creatures

When I looked at Jesus, I saw such compassion. He said, "Come and see this place." And we went to a very black area in the middle of the earth where I heard snakes hissing. The demons there were twelve feet high and twenty feet high. They had three heads and ten arms and ten feet. And oh, were they ugly! They had worms coming out of their wings. And they were everywhere.

I said, "Dear God, what are these?" Jesus told me that what I was seeing was a mixture of illusions of demonic beings and actual demons that attack people. These demons are described in the book of Ephesians as *"principalities,… powers,…rulers of the darkness of this age,…spiritual hosts of wickedness"* (Ephesians 6:12). The evil principalities, powers, rulers, and spiritual hosts work with Satan to lie to people and to deceive them, causing great harm to those who do not know the power of the name of Jesus. The demons seek to destroy Christians by encouraging them to yield to their sinful nature. Whenever we give in to our fleshly desires, we open the door to allow such demons to influence and attack us. But we have power in the name of Jesus and in His blood to counteract these forces of darkness and to stop their evil purposes. We are protected by Jesus' blood as we die daily to our fleshly desires and diligently put on the *"whole armor of God."* (See Ephesians 6:10–18.)

Jesus told me, "You have power to speak My blood over these demonic beings. They're here for a season. As I said, the Father is grieved over the murder and rape of little children, and some of these demons in hell have caused these things and have entered people and possessed them on the earth. It's a horrible thing, My child, but it's all in the hands of God. The people need to know and understand that what God says is true."

As we walked, I heard the Lord say to an evil creature, "Peace, be still." This demonic being looked something like a seal—except that it had about ten legs—and it was rolling in some dust and running. I screamed, "Oh, my God, what's in the middle of the earth?" I hung on to Jesus' hand, and He said, "We're getting close to the abyss." There were slithering snakes there, and I smelled sewage coming down from the earth; the odor reeked of dung and rotten flesh. And again, I heard the cries of multitudes. Over in a black mist with flames of fire, I saw hideous things. I was so afraid. But Jesus was with me and held on tightly to my hand. He said, "Fear not. Nothing will harm you, because you're with Me." About two feet of light appeared around Him, and He pierced the darkness, but I could still see the evil creatures along the wall. They were screaming out blasphemous words to God. I thought, *What in the world?*

The Lord showed me hidden treasures. He moved His hand, and there in the jaws of hell were gold and silver, stacked up like a mountain. He also showed me rivers of blood mixed with fire, in which skeletons were chained together and screaming, "Let us die," and "Help us!" Above them, it said, "Men loving men and women loving women, with no fear of God or His judgments."[11]

Further on, I saw another horrible-looking being with a round face, teeth, and a whispering voice. There were about twenty-five of these creatures. Jesus explained that they planned to go on the earth and cause people to commit suicide, and He told me, "Listen to them." One of them said, "This is what we're going to say to them: 'Oh, nobody loves you. Nobody cares for you. Look at your family—they've

11. See Romans 1:24–27; 3:18.

abandoned you. Look at your friends—you're not good enough for them.'" The demons were discussing how they could weaken people both emotionally and mentally so they would take their own lives. They are lying spirits (see, for example, 2 Chronicles 18:21), and they can cause people to believe deception and delusions. These demons can even make themselves appear and disappear to people, causing these vulnerable people great fear and torment.

Be sober, be vigilant; because your adversary the devil walks about like a roaring lion, seeking whom he may devour. Resist him, steadfast in the faith.   (1 Peter 5:8–9)

"Help Me to Win the Lost"

I have come to the realization that before God's chosen children understand what He has called them to and where they're supposed to be and what position they are to hold, many of them are severely attacked by the enemy. The demons try to get rid of the prophets and apostles and others whom God is raising up. I'm praying that God will bring forth leaders who can explain this deception of Satan to believers and also show them how to prepare for it.

Jesus said to me, "My name, the name of Jesus, and My blood will stop them, Katherine. Tell the people to use My name and renounce suicide demons. Tell them that if they have thoughts of suicide, they should call people who can help them. They should call people to pray for them. Tell them to not be ashamed, for it is not they who are thinking these thoughts; these suicidal ideas are in the airwaves. And tell them I love them and I will help them if they will call on Me."

Jesus turned to me and said, "Katherine, help Me to win the lost. Tell the people what is here. I will anoint the message with truth and the fear of the Lord. Also, I will keep those who turn to Me."

This place was so evil, horrible, and sad. I thought again, *What if it had been me who was brought to hell for eternity, with no more hope, no more destiny, burning forever in pain without being able to sleep or eat or die?* There was no sunlight or rain in hell, just fire and smoke, along with sorrow, grief, fear, and hatred. Men and women from every nation were crying for help, for release, even while realizing they would be in hell forever. Deep sobs of sorrow came from so many. I heard a woman screaming, "I had so many chances to receive Jesus Christ, and I made fun of Him and mocked Him. Then one day I was killed in a car wreck, and I came here. I had the pleasures of sin for a season. Now, it's so sorrowful."

Jesus said, "Tell the people of the earth about this place; tell them to repent before it's too late." Once more, I thought, *Oh, Lord, I hope I don't know any of these souls.* I saw the form of a man. His bones were red and black from burning. He was a very tall skeleton, and in his hands was a book on fire. Jesus stopped and said, "Peace, be still. O man, what are you doing here?" The skeleton turned his head toward Jesus. He had hollowed-out eyes, and snakes were crawling through him. He screamed, "Jesus, can You forgive me now?" And Jesus said, "O man, what did you do?" He answered, "I was called at a young age to preach Your gospel. And I did go to church.

I learned a lot about You. But I never really loved You as I should have. I wanted the world, and I wanted what it could give me, so I lied about You. I told men that men could marry men and that You would love them and understand them, and they would go to heaven. I told people that prejudice was right. I told people we should hate people of other nationalities. I lied. I built a great congregation."

"I Want to Refine My People"

As I looked at this preacher, Jesus said to me, "I want to send the fire that is spoken of in the book of Malachi to refine the people.[12] I want to help them, Katherine, so they'll not end up here like this preacher full of lies who died in his sins. Some of the people you pass by were tricked by him." The refining fire of God is different from the fire in hell. The first is a fire of holiness, which purifies God's people; the second is a fire of punishment.

[God] *will sit as a refiner and a purifier of silver; He will purify the sons of Levi, and purge them as gold and silver, that they may offer to the LORD an offering in righteousness.*   (Malachi 3:3)

"Now, listen," Jesus said. "Come." We began to move out of the jaws of hell and back to my home. Jesus told me, "Katherine, I want to refine My people. I want to send the fire of the Holy Spirit upon them to refine them, the Refiner's

12. See Malachi 3:1–3.

fire. That fire will burn off, destroy, many things of darkness. They don't need to understand it but just believe it. There is coming a time, someday soon, when My children will be more equipped than ever; there is soon coming a day when the movie related to this book will be out, and thousands are going to come to Me, child. I will cause fire to come on My people—not to burn them on the earth but to love them, cleanse them, and bring correction to them and convict their hearts. And they will repent. There are many things I want to do, child."

Jesus continued, "The earth is so big, My daughter, and thousands are dying and going to hell. I am the Waymaker. I am the One who will keep people from a burning hell if they will only turn to Me and repent of their sins. My Father made it easy. Where you saw those wicked demons, and where you saw the valley, and where you saw the river of blood and fire and vapors of smoke,[13] where you saw the demons tormenting those who are dead but yet alive, Satan knows all about this. The prince of the power of the air,[14] the rulers of demon darkness, the spiritual wickedness in high places—tell the people to use My name, Yeshua, the Lord Jesus Christ, Jesus Christ of Nazareth, to come against those things in My name; tell them to plead the blood, My precious blood, over them, and renounce them. I want the youth to arise and to do a book, *How to Cast the Devil Out in Jesus' Name*. I want the youth to understand who I am and what I'm doing. My daughter, this life is as short as the twinkling of an eye, as you well know. The devil is going to release thousands of souls, and I am the Lord your God who is telling you these things."

---

13. See Acts 2:19.
14. See Ephesians 2:2.

Thank You, Lord!

"For behold, the day is coming, burning like an oven, and all the proud, yes, all who do wickedly will be stubble. And the day which is coming shall burn them up," says the LORD of hosts, "that will leave them neither root nor branch. But to you who fear My name the Sun of Righteousness shall arise with healing in His wings; and you shall go out and grow fat like stall-fed calves. You shall trample the wicked, for they shall be ashes under the soles of your feet on the day that I do this," says the LORD of hosts.   (Malachi 4:1–3)

My reader, I love you so much. I do not want you to burn forever in hell with no way out. There are no exits in hell. There are no doors that lead out of hell. When you're there, you stay there, and everything around you is fire, pain, sorrow, grief, and doom, accompanied by the ceaseless cries of souls who want to get out.

Satan wants us to sin with our bodies, so he wars against our hearts and our thoughts. He tempts us to act upon the desires of our fleshly nature instead of living according to God's ways. We must take authority over him and rebuke him in Jesus' name. (See, for example, 2 Corinthians 10:4–6.)

It is time for us to turn back to God. It is time for us to hear what He is saying to us. We don't seem to realize the reason our Savior, Jesus Christ, gave His life on that cruel day in which He was beaten and put upon a cross. He died to keep us from the eternal damnation that I am revealing to you through this book.

Do you care about yourself and other souls? Do you really care? If so, do something about it. Receive Jesus as your Lord and Savior. Tell somebody else about Jesus and how they can be saved through Him. Pray with other people. Satan doesn't want you to open your mouth and speak God's truth. Don't let him stop you. Speak it anyway.

Let us talk about salvation in Jesus Christ! Let us lift up Jesus Christ. He said, *"Now is the judgment of this world; now the ruler of this world will be cast out. And I, if I am lifted up from the earth, will draw all peoples to Myself"* (John 12:31–32).

Recognizing Satan's Deceptions:

Satan wants to deceive people into thinking that things would be better if they took their own life. In reality, he wants to separate them from God and destroy them. The devil also wants people to believe partial truths so they will think they are following God when they are actually being led into error that will pull them away from their heavenly Father. Make sure that you regularly read God's truth, the Bible, and keep your mind focused on what is right and beneficial.

> *Whatever things are true, whatever things are noble, whatever things are just, whatever things are pure, whatever things are lovely, whatever things are of good report, if there is any virtue and if there is anything praiseworthy—meditate on these things.* (Philippians 4:8)

5

Power in the Blood of Jesus Christ

Call Upon Jesus and Be Cleansed

I remember a church service many years ago in which teenagers between the ages of fifteen and eighteen came up to the altar. I preached on drugs and what sin will do to you, and as I spoke, these young people moved toward the front. They were repenting and crying because they were on drugs and doing sinful things. I felt such love and power from God as the teenagers came. It was beautiful.

As they were making their way forward, someone took a picture of them. Later, when I got the film developed, the picture showed something above the teenagers that looked like a reddish blanket coming down out of the ceiling; the red (which I believe symbolized Jesus' blood) became something like water, washing them clean. The Word of God is true. Jesus' blood has never lost its power.

One night, when I was walking with my King down below in hell, the Lord Jesus revealed to me truths about His powerful blood. "My blood was shed upon Calvary to wash away every sin, every evil thing anybody ever committed, the past that was wicked and dirty. If people would repent before Me, I would wash them clean and save their soul, Katherine. But there is something that men, women, and children who know and understand the gospel must do. They must ask Me to forgive them of all their sins and to come into their heart and save their soul. Then My precious blood will wash them clean. When they call upon Me, the angels in heaven know it, and it is exactly as I've said."

If we walk in the light as He is in the light, we have fellowship with one another, and the blood of Jesus Christ His Son cleanses us from all sin. If we say that we have no sin, we deceive ourselves, and the truth is not in us. If we confess our sins, He is faithful and just to forgive us our sins and to cleanse us from all unrighteousness. (1 John 1:7–9)

As Jesus and I began to walk in hell, I looked down at Christ's feet, and the blood was there again. He said, "Child, all of these people we have been seeing would not be here in hell today if they had only believed that My power is still alive today, that My blood is still real today. If they had repented, I would have washed them clean from all their sins and put joy back in their heart and their life; if they had only believed that I am the Son of God." Then He said, "Come and see."

Jesus took me to another place up on the burned path and hillside. Then He raised His arm, and a large door appeared in the atmosphere. Inside, it depicted the lives that many of the burning skeletons had lived on earth. I saw a lot of them in churches, in schools, in towns, and in their cars; they were young people, living everyday lives. "It was the past," Christ said.

Then I heard pastors preach to them in church services, and many of the young people were drawn by the Spirit of God. But when they were out on the street again, they would shake their heads and walk away, not realizing that Satan had a plan in the days ahead to cause them to be in an accident or to die. As I watched this, I saw that many of them didn't have parents who were believers and that they were confused about the teaching they had heard. I said, "Oh, God, it is so simple; You died on that cross to forgive us of all our sins, to heal our broken bodies. You took it all, Jesus. If only they would believe."

Then I saw a few people accept Christ and shout with joy, and the blood of Jesus came down and washed them clean. But I saw others go back into their very sinful ways. And I saw death come to them through car wrecks or other accidents or through gang violence. When I would see them die, I would scream.

One young person died in a motorcycle crash. I watched his soul leave his body; a white mist came out and went up into the air. I saw the outline of his soul, and then I saw black forms come and grab it. And I heard the screams of this soul. The evil spirits pulled it down a gateway into hell, into the fires. They took this soul before the devil, who was sitting on his throne. The devil talked to the demons and showed them on paper where to place the soul in the burning hell.

Tell People About Jesus

I watched similar scenarios over and over, and then I cried out to Jesus, "I can't take it anymore. I can't stand this anymore, Jesus. Help them; do something." He turned to me and said, "Child, what are you going to do? Are you going to tell people about My blood, that if they would repent, it would wash them clean? For you know that in this hour and this time, many are dying and going to hell with false teachings. There is a phantom in the land, My daughter, of people not teaching the truth about My blood, My crucifixion, and My life-giving to save people from eternal damnation in hell. Stand tall and tell them about My blood and about how I gave My life. Tell them how My Father raised Me from the dead. Tell them, tell them, tell them."

At another time, Jesus had showed me skeletons clothed in fire, and He told me, "This is the judgment of the youth who have died on the earth in the last few years." There are absolutely no babies or little children in hell, but there is an "age of accountability" in which young people understand who God is and are capable of making a decision to believe in Him or not. Black chains were wrapped around these skeletons, and they were screaming, "Is there no relief? Can I not die?" They would grit their teeth and say, "Why didn't I listen to my mother? Why didn't I listen to my father? Why didn't I listen to the preacher?" One screamed, "Why didn't my neighbor take me to church? Why didn't somebody tell me about eternal damnation?" Another screamed in a man's voice, very loudly, "The preacher lived right next door to me and never came and told me to repent. I was mean, I was wicked, but no one told me to stop." Then I heard the voice of a young girl who said, "I was demon possessed; I served the devil, and then one day I was killed and came here, and I've been here ever since. Why didn't I listen? I heard about Jesus, and I didn't believe like other people believed. But I served Satan because I believed Satan. Oh, let me die, let me die."

Now the Spirit expressly says that in latter times some will depart from the faith, giving heed to deceiving spirits and doctrines of demons, speaking lies in hypocrisy, having their own conscience seared with a hot iron…."

(1 Timothy 4:1–2)

Pray for Your Family

The blood of Jesus Christ can save your soul from eternal damnation if you will only repent and believe that He shed His blood and died to make you whole. We all come into this world as innocent babies, and we need Christian parents who can teach us about the Lord. But many parents aren't Christians yet. They need to attend a good church, learn about Jesus, and be saved. Then they can teach their children how to be saved.

Pray for your own family. Warn your children, your parents, and your grandparents about hell. Tell them of spiritual realities that they don't know about, and let the Spirit of God draw them to salvation. Don't just ignore their spiritual state and allow them to die without Christ and go to hell.

Recognizing Satan's Deceptions:

Satan wants people to think that just knowing about Jesus and what He did for us on the cross is enough. Yet we have to personally respond to Him and His sacrifice for us in order to be saved. We must believe that He died for us and that His blood is real and powerful and able to cleanse us from all our sin. If you have not yet done that, you can do so right now by praying this prayer:

Dear Jesus,

I believe that You died on the cross for me. I repent of every sin I have committed. Thank You for shedding Your blood to cleanse me of all my wrongdoing. Thank You for washing me clean by Your blood. I believe that God the Father raised You from the dead, and that You have given me new life in You. Fill me with Your Spirit and help me to live for You. In Jesus' name, amen.

6

Jesus Talked with the Dead

When Christ and I were walking together in hell, I was very much afraid, especially when He would go to different levels, different degrees of fire, and talk with various skeletons, who looked like the skeletons you see at Halloween. Many of these souls would get on their knees and beg and cry, but without tears. They would tell Christ things like, "Oh, Jesus, if only I had repented before I died. Now there's no more hope. There's no more destiny for me except eternal damnation."

Eternal Realities

One time, when I was watching Jesus talk with one of the skeletons, I was thinking hard about eternity. Many people on earth continue to go their own way, serving their flesh—their sinful desires that go against God's laws and truth. They keep rejecting God's commandments to repent and be born again through Jesus Christ. Instead, they laugh and mock God. But one day, death will come to them, and if they have not made their life right with God, they will be eternally punished.

Chapter 5 of the book of Galatians talks about the lusts of the flesh. Here is a passage from that chapter:

> For you, brethren, have been called to liberty; only do not use liberty as an opportunity for the flesh, but through love serve one another. For all the law is fulfilled in one word, even in this: "You shall love your neighbor as yourself." But if you bite and devour one another, beware lest you be consumed by one another!
> (Galatians 5:13–15)

Those who practice the works of the flesh without repenting will not inherit the kingdom of heaven; they will inherit hell. (See Galatians 5:19–21.) I remember being with Jesus in many sections of hell where multitudes were screaming to die but could not. Jesus would turn to me and say, "Child, if they had only listened. I am the way, the truth, and the life." Many of the souls would blame other people—they might have been talking about you or me—for not warning them about hell, not telling them about Jesus, not sharing how they could be saved.

The Stories of the Dead

As I walked with Jesus one night, He said, "Come, child, I'm going to show you some things I've not revealed to you yet. They are very sad and horrible, and they break My heart, child; it hurts to see these things, but they must be told so that the earth will awaken and come back to God."

The ground was cracked, burned, dry, and hot—so hot that there were molten rocks on the sides of the pathway. Demons were hiding behind rocks and making awful sounds. Most of the time, these evil spirits were very visible in hell, unlike on earth, and I pondered that fact. After a while,

Christ said to me, "Child, look." We were in a place that appeared old, rusty, dirty, and black. The cries of the dead—the moans, the groans, and the gnashing of teeth—were all around us. And Christ said, "I'm going over here to talk to someone. Come with Me."

We walked over to a walled area and soon came upon a small compartment, or cell; then we came to another, and another. It was a very long line of cells built by demons. Each one had black bars with a big lock on the outside. The floor consisted of dirt and filth. Jesus went up to one of the cells, and I heard the cry of a man's voice. He came over to the bars with his chains rattling. I thought at first that the noise was his bones clinking, but it was the chains, which were wrapped all around him. Where his eyes should have been, there were burned sockets. Part of his foot was missing. He put his bony hands on the bars and cried, "Jesus, Jesus." As he spoke, I saw his greyish-black soul move up and down inside his ribcage. Jesus said, "O man, what is your name and what have you done to be here?" He answered, "Jesus, if I had only, only listened to the gospel. I wanted the world more than I wanted You. I did evil things in the world. I was very wicked. I harbored hatred and unforgiveness, and I killed several people. And I was told on the earth by preachers and other people that You would forgive me, but I didn't believe them. Oh, if I'd only believed. Oh, if I'd only believed. One day, I went to do something, and I was captured by these other wicked people. They put chains around me, and I died in the chains, Lord. They left me tied up in the woods. And here I am in hell with the chains still upon me, and I cannot die. I died on the earth, but when my soul came out of my body, demon powers brought me down a gateway, and I've been here for so many years, Lord. But I can remember every time the gospel was preached to me. I remember every time I heard the good news."

He who believes in Him is not condemned; but he who does not believe is condemned already, because he has not believed in the name of the only begotten Son of God.
(John 3:18)

I looked at Jesus and saw great tears fall down His face. And I heard the moans of another man who was in the next cell. We walked over there, and Jesus said to this skeleton form, the same as He had to the other soul, "O man, what is your name and what have you done to be here?" The voice was deeply sorrowful as it said, "Jesus, I'm here because of lies and deceiving people to get their money. I'm here because I heard the gospel many times and rejected it and loved my life of sin." As he talked, written words appeared around him in the air. They read, "Deceiveth their own self, deceivers and being deceived."[15] The man continued, "Jesus, I had so many chances to repent. I knew the gospel, but I also knew that as long as I lied and manipulated people, because they were so stupid, I could make myself millions of dollars. But the day came when I was killed in a car wreck. I didn't have time to repent. My soul came out of my body, and demons brought me here. And oh, how I've suffered for my sins. And there's no end to it, my God. I know there's no more hope for me." The skeleton shook with a great cry of pain.

---

15. See 2 Timothy 3:13.

I walked on with Jesus, and I felt so sad for all these souls who had loved wicked things and done things that are unspeakable, and I kept on thinking, *Dear God, when will this ever end?*

Do not love the world or the things in the world. If anyone loves the world, the love of the Father is not in him. For all that is in the world—the lust of the flesh, the lust of the eyes, and the pride of life—is not of the Father but is of the world.

(1 John 2:15–16)

I couldn't stop crying. Christ was holding my left hand, and He said, "Come on, child." I looked down at His feet, and every so often where the nail scars were, blood would gush out, and then it would quickly disappear. I thought, *Oh, Jesus, You hurt, You bled, You died for these people, and Your Father raised You from the dead, and You are alive evermore to give us life eternal. If people would only believe the gospel, they would not come to this horrible place.*

There were innumerable cells, with moans and cries coming from every one of them. I said, "God, this is unbearable to me. Can we just please leave?" Jesus looked at me with great tenderness, "There is more I have to show you."

I looked around and wept, and we continued walking among cells. We came to the voice of a woman who was screaming, "Jesus, Jesus, Jesus, I'll now do what is right, if You'll let me out of here. Jesus, Jesus, come hear my story."

Jesus walked over to her and said, "Peace, be still. O woman, what are you here for?" When He said, "Peace, be still," the demons that were nearby fled backward. Light would appear wherever Jesus was talking to someone, and the demons would flee from it. But I knew the word *peace* had also driven them away. The demons didn't ever hear such a word in hell; it scared them, so they ran from it. There is no peace in hell.

This woman said to Jesus, "I was a seller of fine clothes. I bought and sold fine clothing for women. But I had a team of people, too—in the secret, in the dark—that worked witchcraft and spells on the innocent. I used the clothing line only to work my magic. And my magic came back on me. A lot of the Christians know about the power in Your name, Jesus, and the power of the blood that You shed as the Lamb of God. I was no fool. I understood. But my heart was deceived. As I served Satan, I kept thinking he would give me a kingdom. I kept thinking that if I practiced magic and wizardry on the innocent, I would gain more power with the devil, because I enjoyed seeing people suffer."

I looked closely at this soul as she talked to Jesus. Her skeleton seemed afloat, but her chains held her down. Inside her carcass, her soul was a black, dirty mist, but she could move her skeleton mouth as she spoke. Snakes came out of her eyes and through her skeleton form, and worms teethed on her bones, as they did on the bones of all the other souls.

As I listened to her, I thought, *How can this be? She's still thinking of serving the devil as she's burning in hell.* Then, suddenly, fire came around her feet; it shot up over her like a torch, and she screamed, "Stop, O Satan, stop. I served you faithfully on the earth, and this is what you give me?" Her cell actually shook, and Jesus and I walked away. I said, "Jesus, she's still trying to be evil in hell!" The Lord said, "She was highly deceived, mightily deceived by the devil. I would have forgiven her if she'd only come to Me and really meant it. But she didn't really mean it, child. She wanted to play games with Me, games with the devil. And the day came when I stopped drawing unto her. For it says, 'My Spirit will draw them unto salvation.'[16] But there's also a day when a line is drawn, and the judgment of My Father comes."

I walked on with many unanswered questions, really puzzled. And Jesus turned to me and said, "Child, you will understand someday. Right now, I must show you hell."

Do not be deceived, God is not mocked; for whatever a man sows, that he will also reap. For he who sows to his flesh will of the flesh reap corruption, but he who sows to the Spirit will of the Spirit reap everlasting life.
(Galatians 6:7–8)

Before It's Too Late

We traversed a narrow pathway and came to a flat area where the ground was full of hot smoke. Over it was something like dirty, mucky water—it wasn't really water; it was like dung, and there were nasty, filthy smells. The odor was horrifying; it was like the smell of burning plastic, animal dung, and pollution, and it seeped down from the earth. From a distance, I saw infernal, blazing fires. I saw a slow fire creeping on the

16. See John 6:44.

ground and burning things up. I thought perhaps that some of this fire was for the purpose of purifying the ground. I don't know; there were some things I never got answers for.

Jesus said, "Come, child." He caused light to shine, and we began to walk on big, smooth stones across that disgusting place. When we got to the other side, Jesus said, "I want to show you a monster." I thought, *Oh, God.* But He said, "I have you by the hand. I'm with you; fear not." He held my hand with His right hand, and He raised His left hand over the mucky, evil place that we'd just crossed, and the whole thing rose up in the "air" of hell. As it did, I saw that it was actually a huge, ugly monster with enormous eyes, a long tail, and fire coming out of its mouth. It looked like a long dragon with old scaly skin like an alligator's.

I was trembling as I stood next to Jesus, and again He said, "Fear not. It cannot touch you. But in the days ahead, not many will understand that after My church is raptured out, this thing will come up out of hell and roam the earth. But, according to God's Word, it cannot be released until the time spoken by God.[17] For God is the Creator of all things; God is the One."

I still trembled, and I walked close to Jesus. We climbed the hill, and the monster laid back down in the muck. I thought, *Hell is in the middle of the earth. It's the abode of the dead; there are demonic beings, talking skeletons, burning flesh, smells of dung, corruption everywhere.*

I looked up and saw dark objects falling through an opening, falling way down into a valley, and demons were laughing and hurrying toward them. Jesus said, "Child, those are souls who just died on the earth and came down some gateways,

17. See 2 Thessalonians 2:1–12.

and they're going to be picked up by the demons and put in their place of torment. If they were liars, they will be put with liars; if they were murderers, they will be put with murderers; if they were haters, they will be put with haters; if they were unforgiving, they will be put with the unforgiving; if they were drunkards, they will be put with drunkards. They will be placed with thousands such as they. They'll be in pain and sorrow and grief and crying, and they won't be able to get out of here. If they had returned to Me, I would have forgiven them the sins of the flesh. That's why I am showing you hell, to make people turn around and come back unto Me before it's too late, before they reach the everlasting fire."

Jesus was sad, and I was sad. Jesus' hands and feet were bleeding, and He said, "I died for all of these, but it's too late, too late." He looked up and prayed, "My Father, My Father, have great mercy." And hell shook again.

I clung to Jesus and said, "This could have been me when I was backslidden from You, Lord. I was backslidden at one time and did things I shouldn't have. But I repented and came back to You." He looked at me and said, "Child, we are going to go to another place. And in this other place, you're going to see people who kept putting Me off, saying, 'Not yet. Tomorrow, tomorrow.' But tomorrow never came."

Come now, you who say, "Today or tomorrow we will go to such and such a city, spend a year there, buy and sell, and make a profit"; whereas you do not know what will happen tomorrow. For what is your life? It is even a vapor that appears for a little time and then vanishes away. Instead you ought to say, "If the Lord wills, we shall live and do this or that." But now you boast in your arrogance. All such boasting is evil. (James 4:13–16)

We left that place and went around a bigger corner at the bottom of the hill. There were smoldering fires and heat like you would not believe. There was the smell of rotten, burning flesh and dung. There were rats running everywhere. There were snakes, which fled from the presence of Jesus. There were also little bitty things full of hair that were bouncing on the ground; I didn't know what they were, but I was terrified of them.

It is my responsibility to warn you to turn back to God if you have not yet repented of your sins and received Jesus, because the Bible says that if you see the sword coming against the land and you don't warn the people, their blood will be on your hands. (See Ezekiel 33:1–6.) So, I'm telling you like it is. Repent, O earth, repent. Because Jesus is coming back for a church that has no *"spot"*—meaning that we must be cleansed from sin and begin to obey God—*"or wrinkle"*—meaning that we can't just do anything we want to with no fear of God or His commandments. (See Ephesians 5:27.)

You need to read your Bible, and you must hear what the Spirit is saying to the churches. I urge you to faithfully attend a good church that will teach you the truth of God's Word. We must bring back the "ark of the covenant," meaning the holy Word of God, for hell is getting fuller every day with those who have rejected God, those who have rejected

Jesus Christ and the truth of the gospel. Hell is expanding itself while some preachers on earth are lying about the truth. I'm warning the preachers, too: You must repent and turn back to God and help to save people from judgment in hell. If you're not being truthful with them about God's Word, if you're not being real with them, then you're sending many of them to eternal condemnation.

As I continued walking with the Lord, I was becoming angry with the devil, and so was Jesus. I kept thinking, *For all of these down here, there's no tomorrow except for burning pain. All of these down here will be thrown into a lake of fire. Oh, my God, have mercy, have mercy.* I was thinking of all these people. I looked behind me, and there were fires, the screams of the dead, and echoing chambers of horror. I remembered those who had died with diseases and were suffering from them ten times worse in hell, screaming to die from the pain.

A Great Move of God's Spirit

Jesus said, "Come, I want to show you something." We came to a place where there were a great number of men. They were skeletons, but I knew that they were all men because they were screaming in men's voices in languages of every nation. Jesus said, "Look, these all died as alcoholics; they loved strong drink more than they loved Me. They loved to party; they loved to get drunk. They enjoyed their life; they did not really care about anybody but themselves and what made them feel good. There are thousands of alcoholics in the earth yet today. They need to turn back to Me. I'll forgive them and deliver them.

"I'm going to begin to send My Spirit into the earth, Katherine, in a stronger way; I'm going to begin to give chances to many people who are being prayed for by their parents and the church. I'm going to begin to pour out My Spirit of drawing unto them, for the goodness of the Lord draws man unto salvation.[18] I'm going to begin to pour out My Spirit in a unique way that will amaze many people. For hell is getting so full of the people's sins of the flesh that this must be preached about again. People must know that I will deliver them from every sin of the flesh, if they will ask Me. Sometimes I deliver them even if they don't ask, daughter, I truly do, because of My great love for humanity. There is a time and a season coming soon when there will be a great move of My Spirit to bring people unto Me. There'll be a time coming soon when there will be a great avalanche of healings again in the earth, a great revival. And part of the revival will be brought about through what I'm telling you, and a movie will be made out of this book. I will do it, and it is time for this, saith the Lord. It is time for the world to awaken so that people will not come to this horrible place."

Then Jesus said to me, "It's time to go back now. We have been here for quite a while." And I was so glad, because I was very tired and scared. But from time to time during the night, Jesus had touched me and said, "Peace, My child," and great peace had flooded over me. Now, Jesus said, "Let's go," and in the twinkling of an eye, I was out of hell. Jesus moved so fast; He had so much power, and He came down outside my home, and I was still in the spirit. He made sure by His power that I was back in my bedroom, and then He left. I sat up in bed in my human form, and I began to weep.

It is difficult for me to talk about what I experienced in hell. It is hard to describe it. Because of this difficulty, I ask you to pray for me that this truth might go around the world. And if you do not know the Lord Jesus Christ as your

18. See Romans 2:4; Hosea 11:4.

Savior, may you truly repent now of your sins and ask Him to forgive you, come into your heart, and save your soul. Give your life to Him and ask Him to baptize you with His Holy Spirit.

God's Spirit will help you. When you're tempted to commit a sin of the flesh, the Holy Spirit will give you the strength to resist. Call upon God when you are tempted and in trouble, and He will deliver you. If you should fall, He will pick you up again. Do not be afraid to go back to your heavenly Father, and do not harden your heart. Return to Him, and He will forgive you.

Call upon Me in the day of trouble; I will deliver you, and you shall glorify Me.
(Psalm 50:15)

Recognizing Satan's Deceptions:

Satan deceives some people into thinking that if they serve him and worship him, he will reward them with good things in this life and with a kingdom in the next life. His promise of a kingdom is a lie; it is merely an imitation of Jesus' promise that our heavenly Father will give us His kingdom. Satan just wants to use people for his own purposes before discarding and destroying them. They will not receive any "special treatment" from Satan in hell but will suffer eternally. If you have been involved in the occult or if you are currently a follower of Satan, go to God immediately and repent. He will forgive and cleanse you in Jesus. Only God fulfills His promise to give us His kingdom.

But seek the kingdom of God, and all these things shall be added to you. Do not fear, little flock, for it is your Father's good pleasure to give you the kingdom. Sell what you have and give alms; provide yourselves money bags which do not grow old, a treasure in the heavens that does not fail, where no thief approaches nor moth destroys. For where your treasure is, there your heart will be also. (Luke 12:31–34)

Part 2:

Reclaiming the Keys and Gifts of God

7

Keys to the Kingdom

Sound the Alarm

I was walking with Jesus again in the middle of the earth where hell is. Christ was wearing the long white robe, with sandals on His feet. He had the most beautiful, sweet anointing about Him, and such love flowed from Him. But there was a very sorrowful look on His face, and there was deep grief in His eyes. To His left, down in a valley, skeletons on fire were screaming. Straight ahead, there were some pits and cells where skeletons were burning and screaming. Demons were laughing at them and jeering, "We deceived you; we deceived you."

I held tightly to Jesus' hand. We kept walking until we came again to that parched, burned, dry mountain that was very wide and rocky and had many paths on it. Jesus would always make a light shine to show me something. He raised His arm, and we stopped when a large opening appeared in the darkness to our right. Jesus said, "Child, warn My people. Sound an alarm in My holy mountain. Warn them of this place. Tell them what I am showing you and telling you. My

Word will back it all up. These are revelations given from My Father to you that you can tell the world. And now, look, listen, and learn."

Blow the trumpet in Zion, and sound an alarm in My holy mountain! Let all the inhabitants of the land tremble; for the day of the Lord is coming, for it is at hand.

(Joel 2:1)

Bind the Enemy

In the large opening, I saw many demons. They were of various sizes, from about two feet tall to fifteen feet tall. Some of the tall demons had horns on their heads; big, broad faces; and large teeth and fangs. They had huge, hairy bodies and long, clawlike hands, with something like razorblades on the back, and large legs and feet. Some of these demons had three heads. Some demonic beings had six feet, some had three, some had two, and some had one. Some had one arm, some had two, and others had six. Some demons had six wings, while others had ten. Some were shaped like a long, slinky tail with what looked like sharp razorblades. Some were in the shape of a snake and had wings that looked like a snake's head; they had evil-looking eyes and fangs, and fire came out of their mouths.

I shivered and said, "Jesus, why are You showing me this?" He said, "This is Satan's kingdom, child. He works in darkness; he seduces. He sends out demons to bring drugs and alcohol and abuse to families. That is why I gave you My name, the Lord Jesus Christ—so that you could take authority and bind these things; and they shall be bound in chains."

As I watched one of the demons, a big black fiery chain came out of nowhere and bound it. The demon screamed and fell over and could not move. The other demons ran away. Jesus said, "One of My children on the earth is binding this demon with My name, the name of Jesus Christ." The chained demon became covered with flames, and it was reduced to ashes. I said, "Lord, it was cremated." He said, "Yes, and I want them all cremated. But come." We walked past the ashes of that evil demon, and a hot wind came and blew the ashes away. (See Malachi 4:3.)

[Jesus] said to them, "I saw Satan fall like lightning from heaven. Behold, I give you the authority to trample on serpents and scorpions, and over all the power of the enemy, and nothing shall by any means hurt you. Nevertheless do not rejoice in this, that the spirits are subject to you, but rather rejoice because your names are written in heaven."
(Luke 10:18–20)

I kept walking with my King, but I was weary. I was thinking of all the demons I had seen, and I shivered again. The cartoon artists that depict demons don't even know what they are drawing. There are so many seducing powers upon the earth.

Jesus said, "Look, listen, and learn." He raised His arm again, and a large opening appeared, but this time I could see on the earth. I saw the inside of a large grocery store with people pushing shopping carts. I saw families there. All at once, large demons materialized around some of the people. One of them took a woman over to the liquor section; it kept whispering in her ear, "Get this; you know you want this. It would make you feel good to drink it." She would shake her head no and keep on walking. Then a larger demon stood in front of the cart, stopped it, and whispered to her some other things. She went back and bought the liquor. Jesus told me that these demons work in ones, twos, threes, fours, fives, and sixes—different ones at different times to seduce people to get into sin and to destroy their lives and their families.

Then Jesus showed me another part of the vision in which a lot of cars were backed up on a freeway. He zeroed in on one man's car in which there were three demons. One demon whispered, "Well, just drive around them and get out of this mess." In another car, a larger demon was laughing and telling the driver, "Well, I would like to just run over every one of them and kill them." And then I saw the two cars pull out and collide. The cars flipped over, and the drivers died. I thought, *Oh, my God, the seducing power of these tongues of darkness, these words of evil.* I said, "We must obey the laws of the land. Our world would be chaos if we didn't have laws of the land."

Then I was taken in the Spirit with Jesus. We seemed to be at a bar on the earth. Jesus let me see inside to the barstools. Demons were sitting around in the darkness, and they were whispering to the men, "Buy more alcohol and get arguments going." These demons appeared to go in and out of some of the men, and I wondered why. And there were women there, too. Jesus said, "They've opened the door to the enemy to do whatever he wants to with them." I thought, *Oh, my God*. Then He said, "They will all end up in hell, My daughter, if someone doesn't warn them. They need to repent and turn to Me, and I will deliver them and protect them by My Word and My covenant and My blood."

Again, I would challenge you to attend a good church that teaches you the holy Word of God and to keep yourself from evil.

After this, Jesus and I were walking in hell on ground that was very cracked and burned. We stopped, and I saw many flames shooting up, as well as cells. Jesus said, "Look." When I looked at the cells, I saw the people who had crashed their cars on the freeway. I saw the woman who had been in the grocery store. I also saw people from other scenes that I had watched. For a few minutes, those souls seemed to have flesh so that I could recognize who they were. Then the flesh turned into bones, and there were worms on the bones, and I heard the screams of these dead souls. They were saying, "Why didn't somebody warn me? Why didn't somebody tell me of this place?"

The Lord looked at me and said, "Katherine, you are to warn people. You are to tell them of this place called hell. Many demonic devices are used against people. And I have given you the authority to bind the devil, to loose My power upon the people, to set the captive free. I am anointing you with a new anointing to share this new revelation. I'm anointing you with more power, My daughter, to set the captive free."

[Jesus said,] ***"The Spirit of the Lord is upon Me, because He has anointed Me to preach***

*the gospel to the poor; He has sent Me to heal
the brokenhearted, to proclaim liberty to the
captives and recovery of sight to the blind, to
set at liberty those who are oppressed."*

(Luke 4:18)

My heart goes out to people who are being held captive by the devil. I looked at Jesus and said, "Thank You, my Lord, thank You, thank You." We kept walking, and I was thinking, *Well, Jesus, I've made mistakes. How can You even use me?*

All at once, the Lord stopped, looked at me, and said, "Katherine, My Father has chosen you, and I have chosen you. You are washed in My blood; you are cleansed by My blood. You are clean through My Word. I do not want you to be concerned about the past, for it is gone. We must look at tomorrow and have hope, My daughter, great hope."

Keys for Releasing the Captives

Jesus said, "Now I want to show you a place of different layers and degrees for different torments of souls for the various works of the flesh they committed upon the earth. Some of them were murderers. Some were thieves. Some were robbers. Some were liars. I can make people overcome these things if they would accept Me as Lord and Savior, if they would give Me their heart and would love Me with all their mind, their soul, and their strength. There is much that I have for the people, Katherine. I am showing you the abode of the dead and the reasons they are here, and I am showing you that I am the way, the truth, and the life. If any man comes to Me, I will in no wise cast him out.[19]

"I am showing the people through revelations how to pray and use My name and pull down strongholds and shut doors of evil. Many years ago, My daughter, I appeared to you in a burning bush in Guatemala. There are so many things I want to teach the people about the keys to the kingdom. The keys to the kingdom are: 'Whatever you bind on earth is bound in heaven. Whatever you loose on earth is loosed in heaven.'[20] And there are many other keys." I said, "Thank You, Jesus, for those teachings. Thank You for this revelation. Thank You, Lord."

Jesus gave us the keys to the kingdom so that we could take dominion and authority over the powers of darkness and thereby set the captives free. Many times, I have been ministering in a service when God's anointing has come in very powerfully, and people have been screaming and seeking Christ. The people have told me that God touched them and set them free. I open up this revelation knowledge so that people can understand how to use the keys to the kingdom to release the captives.

In a mighty supernatural visit, the Lord revealed to me further keys to the kingdom. The more I think about them and study them, I believe that the keys to the kingdom are similar to the various fruits of the Spirit of God. (See Galatians 5:22–23.) In addition to the keys of binding and loosing and using the authority of Jesus' name, some other keys are:

---

19. See John 6:37 (KJV).
20. See Matthew 16:19; 18:18.

- Obedience—obeying God and doing whatever He tells us to do. If we fail, we are to get right back up, repent, ask for forgiveness, and keep going.

- Compassion—showing true concern for the lost, sick, and oppressed.

- Humility—having a humble spirit before God.

- Love—loving other people as God has loved us.

As we obey God, have great compassion on people, humble ourselves in God's sight, and love others, then miracles, signs, and wonders will occur.

Then Jesus went about all the cities and villages, teaching in their synagogues, preaching the gospel of the kingdom, and healing every sickness and every disease among the people. But when He saw the multitudes, He was moved with compassion for them, because they were weary and scattered, like sheep having no shepherd. Then He said to His disciples, "The harvest truly is plentiful, but the laborers are few."

(Matthew 9:35–37)

The Lord said to me, "Katherine, many souls would not be in hell if they had listened and used the keys to the kingdom. If many of My ministers would take heed to their lives, stop doing the things the world is doing, and turn unto Me with all their heart, their mind, their soul, and their strength, thousands would be saved from this place. Truly, there is more teaching on the keys to the kingdom. But let's move on, daughter."

Quicksand in Hell

Jesus and I began to walk again, and we came to a very large area that was full of different degrees of fire, with skeletons of every size. There was weeping and gnashing of teeth. Worms were coming out of the skeletons' bones. I watched the souls scream and pull out some of the worms.

When we arrived at this group of skeletons—there must have been two thousand of them—I saw that they had black chains around their ankles, and that they were also chained to one another. Flames came around them, engulfed them, and went over their heads. The flames would die down and then come again. The skeletons were standing on something like quicksand, because every so often, some of them would sink below the surface and then bob back up again.

As the flames burned their bones, the skeletons would scream and cry, "Help me; does anybody care about my soul? Help me; I cannot die. Why was I not warned of this place? Why was I not told of this place of eternal damnation?"

I watched in horror as demons stood around this large place. The area seemed to be like a dried-up lake, but it was moist and damp where the skeletons were. I looked more closely and saw that some skeletons would sink to their waist before they came back up, while others would sink to their neck before rising again. Their screams and the cries of the other dead were beyond belief.

I thought, *Oh, my God, what terrible things drugs and alcohol, perversion, uncleanness, and all the works of the flesh do to people; and yet these fires are God's eternal judgment, the fires of God that will never go out.* (See Mark 9:43–48.) I watched in shock as other demons would drag souls to a high cliff and throw them in the quicksand, which added to the cries of the dead. I wondered, *Oh, my God, what torment is this? What torture is this, Jesus?* Jesus looked at me and said, "My daughter, behold, I gave My Word, I gave My name, I gave My blood. I gave instructions in My holy Word. I have great preachers and leaders in the lands. And yet, many people still love their evil ways—their carousing, fighting, drinking, swearing, blaspheming, and speaking evil of all things and all men. I plead with them and plead with them to stop, but they do not. And this is the end for some of them; this is the place of the judgment of God for some men and women who have gone a different way. They loved the lust of their own flesh more than God's commandments. Men loving men and women loving women.

"Many cries have come out for people in the earth to repent, as with Sodom and Gomorrah; some have and some haven't. But, if you notice, as these souls come up out of the quicksand, they are chained together, and they are hitting each other and screaming at each other with their bony arms and hands. They are nothing but skeletons full of dead men's bones. They scream because of their sins, yet they still desire to do evil; but they cannot."

Woe is the man who will not listen to God's Word, I said to myself. *Woe is the woman who will not take heed to correction.* As I looked again at these masses, over two thousand or more souls clothed in fire and being sucked down into the quicksand,

I thought, *Oh, my God, we need to warn people; we need to tell them of this awful place.* I remembered that the book of Romans says that God gave people over to a debased mind because they rejected Him and did not want to retain a knowledge of Him. (See Romans 1:18–32.) As I watched, I thought of how many thousands of people in the world were in that state.

Today, certain laws in our lands have changed greatly for the worse. The truth of Jesus Christ must be preached more and more to save people from a horrible hell. I believe we must love people, counsel them, and guide them, so that perhaps they will turn from their sins and call out to God. We must stand firm for the counsel of God and try to win even murderers to Him. People must understand the role and deceit of demons, although self-willed people sometimes do wicked things even when no demons are involved. We must use the keys to the kingdom to set people free.

I bow in my heart to Jesus. I love Him, and I know there is a price to pay to be alone with Him, for the enemy does not want us to spend time with Jesus, learning from Him, believing in His Word, and coming to understand His supernatural power.

I looked up at my Savior, and the expression on His face was one of great pain. As He observed the judgment of His Father upon lost souls, His eyes were so sad. Jesus said to me, "If only they had listened, they would not be here. If only they had understood that I did everything for them so they could have life eternal in heaven with Me. Come on, child, I want to show you something else."

God so loved the world that He gave His only begotten Son, that whoever believes in Him

should not perish but have everlasting life.
For God did not send His Son into the world
to condemn the world, but that the world
through Him might be saved.

(John 3:16–17)

Devouring Serpents

We began to walk along a curved pathway, and I could hear the cries of the dead far into the blackness. I wondered where Jesus was taking me, and I held His hand tightly. I was so afraid. I thought about my family on the earth, wondering, *How are they going to believe me?* I thought about passages in the Bible that talk about how God will protect us and watch over us.[21] I thought about how I wanted Jesus to return to earth very quickly.[22] Yet, as I walked there in hell among the dead, I also thought about the millions of people on the earth who didn't know Jesus and how I had a big responsibility to release this deep revelation of hell to the world.

When we came to a high cliff, I looked around. There was darkness, then light, and then fire below us. After that, I saw what looked like another mountain, like a volcano getting ready to erupt. It was red and bulging, and its base looked like charcoal. I looked at the Lord and said, "Jesus, is that going to be an earthquake?" He said, "Yes, child, at the appointed time. My Father is in control of all these things. And He said He wants man to repent and turn unto Him, child."

---

21. See, for example, Psalm 139:7–10.
22. See, for example, Revelation 22:20.

Then Jesus told me, "Look over this way." I was standing on His right side, and I looked far down a high cliff. I was very afraid of heights like that, so I clung to Him and said, "What is this, Jesus?" He replied, "Keep looking in the darkness." I looked far down. As Jesus spoke, light appeared, and I could see a valley in which there were snakes the size of a train. Some were curled up, and others were stretched out. I screamed, "Jesus, what is this?" He said, "These serpents shall be released after My church is caught out.[23] They will be destroyed, but they will devour many before this happens, My daughter." *Oh, God. Oh, God.* I said, "Please stop it; please abort this awful thing." He looked at me with tears in His eyes, and then He moved His arm back, and darkness covered the serpents again. But I could hear snarls, hissing, and even some blasphemy coming from them. I thought, *Oh, my God, how I hate snakes!*

Jesus said, "You have to go home now. I'll take you back now, but tomorrow night I will bring you here again, and I will show you and tell you some things that are very important to the body of Christ and to the world."

Reclaiming the Keys and Gifts of God:

So far, we have noted these keys to the kingdom: (1) binding and loosing, (2) using the name of Jesus, (3) obedience, (4) compassion, (5) humility, and (6) love. Read Galatians 5:22–23 and write down in what ways you think these keys of the kingdom correspond to the fruits of the Spirit. Begin to focus on one particular fruit of the Spirit that you will cultivate in order to better prepare yourself to use the keys to the kingdom.

---

23. See, for example, 1 Thessalonians 4:15–17.

8

Glass-like Cages

Gifts in Captivity

The next night, after Jesus had brought me back to hell, He told me, "Listen, child, there are things that must be unlocked and released from here. Take the keys to the kingdom and unlock these doors with Me." Jesus had many keys with Him. I said, "Okay, what do I do, Lord Jesus?" He said, "Look, listen, and learn."

We walked what seemed like miles around an area that had heaps of skulls and was filled with bad odors. Christ told me to call this area the Cave of Debris. This cave was a revelation; for example, even the dung on the walls represented the corruption of mankind. There was also a large number of containers—perhaps a thousand of them—that looked as if they were made of solid glass.

Suddenly, we stopped walking. I looked more closely at some of these glass containers, and I wondered why the glass looked so clean and why the things inside them looked like holy objects, such as golden horns, drums, robes, crowns, music sheets, and books. I said, "What is this, Lord Jesus?"

He said, "These were gifts I gave to My church and to My people to spread the gospel; the book of First Corinthians talks about the gifts of God."

There are diversities of gifts, but the same Spirit. There are differences of ministries, but the same Lord. And there are diversities of activities, but it is the same God who works all in all. But the manifestation of the Spirit is given to each one for the profit of all: for to one is given the word of wisdom through the Spirit, to another the word of knowledge through the same Spirit, to another faith by the same Spirit, to another gifts of healings by the same Spirit, to another the working of miracles, to another prophecy, to another discerning of spirits, to another different kinds of tongues, to another the interpretation of tongues. But one and the same Spirit works all these things, distributing to each one individually as He wills.

(1 Corinthians 12:4–11)

One glass container had something like pure, beautiful smoke rising from it and then disappearing. Another had fire inside it. I learned that in these containers, each of which had a lock on it, were "trophies" of Satan—things related to the Lord that the enemy had stolen. (I faintly remember having read something similar to this years earlier from someone else who had seen hell, but I don't remember the details.)

Releasing God's Treasures

I was so tired that I leaned on the Lord and said, "Oh, Jesus, what can I do?" He said, "Look, listen, and learn. I've given you the keys to the kingdom. I want you to take a key in your hand in the spirit." All at once, I looked at my hand, and there was a spiritual key in it. "What do I do with it, Jesus?" I asked. He said, "Come with Me." Then we were standing in front of one of the large, transparent, glass-like cages. Something that looked like a white glow was moving in it. I said, "What is this, Lord?" He replied, "Take the key, put it in the lock, and in My name, Jesus Christ, Emmanuel, Yeshua, open that door."

So, in the name of Jesus Christ, Emmanuel, Yeshua, I put the spiritual key in the lock and turned it. The lock broke open, and out flowed the most beautiful presence. Jesus had dropped to His knees, and He said, "My Spirit will once again flow over the earth and bring the people on the earth to conviction. My Spirit will again begin to draw people unto Me, child, by the thousands."

Like a mighty wind, that beautiful presence went up and out of hell; I saw it break through the earth and shout up into heaven. And Jesus said, "It is going to My Father, so that He can purify and cleanse it. The angels will take care of it." We walked toward the next one. I said, "Oh, Jesus, this is going to take forever." And He said, "No, you will see in a few moments."

On top of the next glass cage, which held a crown, was written "The Trophies of Satan." The crown seemed to be alive; it was moving in the air, and it had jewels in it. The Lord said, "This is all spiritual and natural, child. I want to crown My people with glory and with righteousness, but the enemy has sent demons by the thousands, and he has blocked so much of My grace for My people. And I want you to cut away the debris."

As I looked at this beautiful crown, Jesus said, "Take this." And again, a spiritual key appeared in my hand. Then He said, "You do that in My name, Jesus Christ, Yeshua, Emmanuel." I declared, "In the name of Jesus Christ, Yeshua, Emmanuel, be loosed from this place." When I said that, the door of the cage opened. A wind came around the crown, and the crown shot up through hell and straight into the sky above the earth. And I saw God's angels take it and bring it into glory.

We went to a final cage. Due to the fire of Jesus, the ground all around us was being cleansed; the debris was burning away. I was so happy because I no longer smelled foul odors. This last cage also said "The Trophies of Satan." Inside were flaming swords, and a Bible was over them. They were moving as if they were alive. Jesus said, "Here is another key. Now do the same with this one." I said, "In the name of Jesus Christ and Emmanuel, Yeshua's name, I open up this door for the glory of God, in Jesus' name." The door swung open, and then a wind swirled around Christ and me, and we were raised up out of hell, into the sky above the earth, and into the galaxies.

The wind belongs to Jesus. I saw that the flaming swords were suspended in the galaxies. I thought, *Oh, my God, the swords are on fire, and the Word was over them. What is this?* Jesus told me, "It is My Word. My Word will come back again.

The flame, the swords, represent the fire of God. The fire will permeate the darkness and the demons, My daughter." All at once, angels came and took the swords up to heaven. Jesus said, "They will all be cleansed and purified."

Above all, taking the shield of faith with which you will be able to quench all the fiery darts of the wicked one. And take the helmet of salvation, and the sword of the Spirit, which is the word of God; praying always with all prayer and supplication in the Spirit, being watchful to this end with all perseverance and supplication for all the saints.
(Ephesians 6:16–18)

I looked at the Lord and thought, *Jesus, who am I that You would do these things through me?* He answered, "Because I have chosen you, little one. I love you, and I am going re-build your youth. I am going to strengthen you and heal your body. People are going to be amazed at the sign you will be on this earth." I said, "Oh, thank You, God. Thank You. I am so tired, Lord. Oh, Lord, I love You so." Jesus said, "You are going home now, and tomorrow we will come back to the cave, My daughter." Then I was back in my home again.

Jesus had revealed to me that what I had seen that night represented the spiritual and the natural; I was using supernatural keys to change the state of things on earth. I knew that what Satan had brought into captivity must be loosed in the mighty name of Jesus Christ with the keys to the kingdom.

From walking with the King, I knew how important it was to listen to every word He said. As I was thinking about all these things, I understood that the devil had brought much heartache and depression to people, causing them to give up their gifts and permitting him to take the gifts captive. Now these gifts had to be loosed again on the earth.

Reclaiming the Keys and Gifts of God:

What gifts has God given you to build His church and to reach the lost? Are you using them? If not, why? If you have become discouraged, depressed, or even lazy to the point of allowing your gifts to slip away from you through disuse, ask God to forgive you and to restore these gifts to you. In Jesus' name, loose them from the stronghold of the enemy. Then, ask God how He wants you to use these gifts for His glory.

9

God Has Rescued His Glory

The next night, Jesus Christ appeared to me and said, "Child, let's go." We returned to the horrible cave where I had seen the glass cages containing the gifts that Satan had stolen from God's people. As I looked around, I thought about how I had laid down my own gift at times. I hadn't listened to God; I hadn't prayed; I hadn't written. The Lord had shown me and told me many things that I had never recorded or related to other people. I thought, *It is so important to let God use you to the fullest.*

The Restoration of God's Gifts

Jesus and I now looked at another glass cage. Like many of the others, it was labeled "The Trophies of Satan." In it, books and pens were suspended in the air. The pages of the books would open, and I could see that they contained revelation knowledge and wisdom from God. The covers of the books would change from gold to silver. These were books that God wanted people to write, books that were meant to be award winners.

I watched as Jesus told me, "Take the spiritual key." Again, a spiritual key appeared in my hand. He continued,

"Now open this gate in My name." So I put the key in the lock and turned it in the mighty name of Jesus; I commanded the door to open in the name of Yeshua, Emmanuel. When I unlocked the door, again the wind came, and the door flew open. The wind carried the books right out of hell and straight up like a tunnel into the sky. I knew the angels would catch them, cleanse them, and take them to the Father.

I was so excited to know that God was setting free from captivity the gifts that He had given to the church for preaching the gospel of Jesus Christ, for telling people about heaven and hell, and for announcing His coming. I wept a little in my soul, and I thought, *Oh, my God, I am going to be more obedient so that the devil cannot steal the gifts of God.*

I knew that God was going to repair and restore His gifts to His people and that many demonic powers were going to be cremated by God, for it is their judgment time, so that the Word of God can spread over the world and God's glory can return in greater measure to the earth. I *knew* this. The Holy Spirit is my Guide and Teacher, and He is right here with me as I record these revelations for you.

We went to the next glass cage, and I thought, *What is in this one?* Jesus said, "Katherine, what do you think is in here?" At first, I couldn't see anything inside it. Then, when I did see something, I couldn't make out what it was, but it resembled a cloud. So I asked, "Jesus, what is in this glass cage?" He said, "The reason it is in glass and it is transparent is so that Satan doesn't come down here and rejoice when thinking about what he has done with the gifts of God. But this day, they are going to be set free and come back up on the earth, and My Father will purify them."

When I looked into the glass cage, its contents disappeared again, and then I saw something like a blackness and then a whiteness. I thought, *What in the world is this, Jesus?* He told me, "Child, look again, but rebuke that darkness in My name." So I said, "Father, in the mighty name of Jesus, I rebuke this darkness." Suddenly, the darkness fled.

Jesus said, "Child, this is the gift of discernment. Real discernment has been stolen from the earth. This gift is very important to the body of Christ so that people will not be seduced by the devil. This gift is operated by the Holy Spirit, but it was stolen, and the enemy has mixed falsehood with it. He mixes things to bring delusions to people. Now, take a spiritual key and open this door."

I turned the key in the lock and said, "In the name of Jesus Christ, in the name of Emmanuel, in the name of Yeshua, I open this door and loose this gift from this place." The door opened up, and a wind came as before. It was as if there was a gentle breeze around this gift of discernment, and it shot straight up out of the top of the cage and into the sky. Angels gathered it into something like a large glass vase with a cover. I said, "Lord, that is so remarkable." He replied, "It is not by might, nor by power, but by My Spirit, saith the Lord;[24] and I will not allow My Spirit to be mixed with anything false. I am saying that the Spirit of Truth, the Spirit of Revelations, the Spirit of the Gifts of the Spirit will return to the church and to the earth." I let out a big sigh and went on to the next glass cage.

There shall come forth a Rod from the stem of Jesse, and a Branch shall grow out of his

24. See Zechariah 4:6.

roots. The Spirit of the LORD shall rest upon Him, the Spirit of wisdom and understanding, the Spirit of counsel and might, the Spirit of knowledge and of the fear of the LORD.
(Isaiah 11:1–3)

"Lord, what is in this cage?" I asked. He showed me shiny gold and silver guitars. In all, there were twelve cages of musical instruments. Jesus said, "Satan has stolen the real praise of God, the real music. It has to come back. So take the key and open these." I took the spiritual key to one cage and said, "In the mighty name of Jesus, Emmanuel, Yeshua, I loose this." When I turned the key in the lock, the power of God came out, and these musical instruments shot up out of hell into the earth above, and the angels gathered them. The same thing happened with the others, until all twelve cages had been opened by spiritual keys. Sometimes, I said, "In the name of Jesus Christ, Emmanuel, Yeshua, I loose this gift to go back to the Father to be repaired." Jesus would prompt me what to say. He told me, "Child, you are loosening these gifts from the bondage of Satan, and they are going to go back and be replenished." I replied, "Praise ye the Lord. Praise God."

We continued walking and came to many other glass cages; there were so many that they seemed to be without number. I would take the keys and speak what Jesus told me to say. We came to one in which a beautiful satin robe was floating. It was florescent white with gold trim, and red would appear on it at times. It was adorned with diamonds and every other type of precious stone imaginable, as well as pearls. I took the key and said, "In the name of Jesus Christ, Yeshua, Emmanuel, I loose this from the captivity of Satan." After I unlocked the door, the robe shot out, and Jesus shouted! As it went up, there seemed to be a dove flying with it. Jesus told me this was the robe of righteousness. Many of God's people had sold out to sin and fleshly pleasures, and they were not living godly lives, but righteousness would now be restored to the church.

As we went along, we came to a glass cage that held the robe of salvation. In another cage was something that looked like a dove, crying. After we loosed these, we went to a cage containing an outline that looked like the spirit of a person humbly bowing his head and crying. God would not tell me what that was. But Jesus loosed it, and, like all the others, it shot up and out of the top of the cave in a mighty whirlwind, and the angels received it in the air.

For several days, Jesus and I walked among these glass cages. He put the spiritual keys in my hand, and I gladly unlocked the doors. One cage was full of gold and silver, and Jesus said, "Child, Satan has bound up the finances, the money, of many, but My Word is true. I said I will bless; I will restore My people and bring wealth to them so that they can preach My gospel. Take this spiritual key." He put a spiritual key in my hand, and I said, "In the name of Jesus, Emmanuel, Yeshua,…" This time, Jesus told me to add, "…to God be the glory, and to loose this." When I turned the key in the lock, the door flew open. The glory of the Lord is so powerful. A wind came and picked up all the gold and silver and carried it through the top of the cave and into the sky, where there were something like horses with chariots that had a holding place for all this gold and silver. There were riders in the chariots, and they shouted, "To God be the glory!" I thought, *Oh, my goodness, what a vision, what a revelation. The earth needs to know that God is truly setting free His glory.*

For the earth will be filled with the knowledge of the glory of the Lord, as the waters cover the sea. **(Habakkuk 2:14)**

"The Thief Has Been Caught"

I don't know how to put it into words, but when I looked at Jesus, He appeared to have "more." He is full of wisdom and understanding, but somehow He looked even more steadfast. I looked inside another cage and saw that suspended in the air were Bibles from all nations. The Lord said, "Satan has watered down My Word. The thief has been caught, Katherine. With a revelation that I am going to release to the earth, people will know how evil the devil is, and they will begin to cry to Me and look to Me again. Satan has taken their eyes off of Me, and he has brought distorted words."

Jesus gave me a spiritual key, and with that key to the kingdom I unlocked the door in the name of Jesus Christ, Yeshua, Emmanuel. The door flew open, and the wind came and took those Bibles right out of hell and into the sky above the earth. Angels came to retrieve them, just as they had with the contents of all the other cages; the angels had beautiful small glass containers, and they put each Bible inside a glass container and then went up to heaven. The Lord said, "Child, this day, saith the Lord Your God, as you are writing this and

102 A Divine Revelation of Satan's Deceptions

recording this in 2013, great revivals shall begin to break out in the earth because this is being revealed."

We went on to the next glass cage, which was full of fire. Jesus said to me, "Child, all through My Word, it talks about God as a consuming fire. All through My Word, it talks about the Holy Spirit fire, the Holy Spirit presence. It talks about the fire to cleanse things, to purify things. Also, in Malachi, it says that the wicked shall be ashes…." He told me, "Say, 'Ashes.'" I said, "Ashes." Then He continued, "…under the souls of your feet. My saints have not sought Me on that revelation. I gave them the keys. I gave them the fire through the Holy Spirit baptism. In the book of Acts, the fire of God was even enclothed in tongues above the disciples' heads."[25]

"Now, My child, this fire in here has been kept secret. It says 'Trophy of Satan,' for although there are many people in the earth, few have grasped this revelation; but this is the mightiest gift to My children, and the gift of love. And your hearts must be pure; you must live right to be able to use this fire. My daughter, now I will release it, saith the Lord your God, and it will go all over the earth, and it will bring revival. It will burn off the droughts. It will burn up the demon powers. This is their time of judgment; it is now because I went to the cross and shed My blood. Many do not understand this revelation, but they can use My name and ask the Father to send the fire to cremate the darkness, and the Father will."

Jesus paid the high price of being mocked, taking the sins of the world on Himself, suffering death on the cross, and defeating Satan and his demons so that we could use His name, the name of the Lord Jesus Christ, to defeat the enemy. Yet we have neglected to use His name; and we have not understood the

---

25. See Acts 2:1–4.

power of God's fire to destroy the works of the enemy. We must ask the Lord to send His fire to burn up the forces of darkness.

I said, "Oh, Lord, forgive me for not understanding." He said, "The glass cage in which we saw the smoke and the darkness and the light that was released, My daughter, was also for understanding." When I looked at Him, I saw His face light up, and I asked, "Oh, Jesus, You are very happy over this?" And He said, "Yes, take this spiritual key in My name and open this up." I took the key to the kingdom that He had given me, and, in the name of Jesus Christ, Yeshua, Emmanuel, I unlocked the door to this fire, and the door flew open. A high wind came, and it caught up Jesus, me, and the fire, and we went up through the top of the cave, into the earth, above the earth, and into the galaxies, with the earth far below us. Jesus said, "Behold, behold, angels." There were many angels shouting, and they were dancing in fire. Then other angels came and put the fire from the cage into a container.

God makes His angels spirits, His ministers a flame of fire.   (Psalm 104:4)

I saw something like a stairway going up to heaven. And Jesus said, "I must go now, and you have to go home. But I want to tell you something: Very soon, I am going to take you up this stairway to see heaven and to come back and report. It will not be your time to leave the earth. I am going to take you there just for a visit and then bring you back. But now I must go with My angels to My Father and present this before My Father." I thought, *Oh, I'm so happy. This is truly God.* With His finger, Jesus wrote in the sky some Hebrew words I didn't understand. Then I was back in my home, and daylight was coming. I thought, *Oh, my Lord, how beautiful.*

Jesus had said, "The thief has been caught." That meant that the devil had been caught with his trickery, his mockery, his seducing, his taking the gifts of God and mutilating them and mixing them with corruption. But Jesus said that God's fire was being released to burn up much of the enemy's darkness and to give His saints understanding of how to use the fire of the Holy Spirit, the fire of the presence of the Lord. Praise the Lord!

The fire brings cleansing. God has a spiritual fire to destroy the darkness. He has weapons against Satan. He has swords. He has His mighty Word. And we must learn about His gifts and weapons for us. We have to study them and, in the name of Jesus Christ, keep moving forward with them to defeat the enemy. Therefore, read the Bible and study the passages that refer to the spiritual fire of God. (See, for example, Exodus 13:21–22; 24:17; Deuteronomy 4:24; 9:3.) *"For our God is a consuming fire"* (Hebrews 12:29).

The Sleeping Giant

The book of Proverbs says that a thief must return sevenfold what he stole. (See Proverbs 6:30–31.) I think the same applies to what Satan has stolen from the church. God has given us spiritual keys to open spiritual locks and to release what the devil has robbed from us. So, with the wisdom of God, I just want to say this: It is time for us to take back these "trophies" of Satan. It is time for us to arise and use our gifts. It is time for us to stand up with the keys to the kingdom.

We must recognize that we have been far too lazy and apathetic about the things of God. Although the Lord has given us many gifts, we don't want to use them. Sometimes, we are afraid that we will offend somebody if we exercise a gift. My friend, God wants you to arise and serve Him, no matter whom you offend. I prophesy that you will rise up with the gift that He imparted to you, the one that has been buried. I prophesy that you will be as bold as a lion and have the courage to complete the job God has given you to do, because thousands are dying and going to hell—the very hell that I have been describing. There are many souls suffering in eternal punishment today who wish they had been born again, who wish they had obeyed God.

The Lord asks you to unite with Him in defeating the enemy. You must wake up, shake the dust off yourself, and start praying and doing what He has called you to do. There are people reading this book right now who are running from the gift God has given them. Stop, repent, and claim that buried gift in Jesus' name. God wants you to rejoin His army. He will heal your wounds, and He will mortally wound the forces of darkness. I am not referring to people receiving a mortal wound but rather the devil and his demonic spirits. It is time for the church to arise as a powerful army for God in the earth. Let this "sleeping giant" arise in the mighty name of Jesus. Amen!

Reclaiming the Keys and Gifts of God:

Are you running from the gifts God has given you? Are you afraid of offending someone if you use a particular gift? If so, move past your fear by focusing on the ways in which your gift will help other people to grow in their faith, to be healed or delivered, to be

106 A Divine Revelation of Satan's Deceptions

comforted, to be spiritually refreshed, and so forth. Commit your gifts to God and then begin to exercise them in faith. Start using them in small ways, and as you learn how to exercise them under God's guidance, you will gradually be able to use them in greater ways.

We must always remember, too, that our spiritual gifts are to be used in conjunction with the gifts of other believers. We need to work together in Jesus' name to accomplish God's purposes. It takes a corporate anointing to break yokes of demonic bondage off of people. God desires a restoration of unity in the body of Christ. (See, for example, 1 Corinthians 12:12–31.)

10

Arise

In this chapter, I want to talk more about awakening the sleeping giant. The giant is God's people, His army, all over the earth. We've been slumbering for too long. The church must be stirred up again, and its leaders—prophets, apostles, pastors, and others—must pull themselves together, because there are millions of spiritually lost and oppressed people who need us. We have to comprehend the reality of heaven and hell and the significance of our calling to share the gospel. We have been too lazy as time has slipped by and hundreds of thousands have gone to hell.

What if you had just died and, having rejected Jesus Christ, were slipping into hell right now? God has shown me the horrors of eternal punishment, and He has shown those horrors to others, too. He will continue to show them, because He is trying to shake believers awake. I am very serious about this. We must *fight the good fight of faith* (1 Timothy 6:12).

The Chamber of Death

Jesus Christ appeared to me again and, by His power, took me with Him down a gateway to hell. This time, we ended up in an area that was even darker than any I had been in before. Jesus said, "Behold, child, we are in the right arm of hell." He raised His right arm, and a great door appeared in the darkness. Then He spoke, and light shone everywhere. I was able to see things that would just astonish you. They astounded me, and I grabbed the Lord's hand.

Jesus was again wearing a white garment, which was shining and brilliant, a golden belt around His waist, and sandals. His hair was beautiful, and His skin was olive-colored. His eyes pierced through my soul. As I looked at Him, I began to weep, and I said, "Lord Jesus, You died and gave Your life and Your blood to keep us from this place. And what I behold with my eyes is horrible."

I stood close to Him and just cried. He put His arm around me to comfort me and said, "Child, you don't even realize how important you are to My kingdom. You don't realize, do you?" I said, "No, Lord." He said, "I'm glad you are like a child, with a humble spirit of compassion; that you can tell of these things you see without greed, without wanting money."

I looked where Jesus had opened the door in the darkness, and it seemed as if I could see very clearly for a hundred miles. The area inside that door was called the Chamber of Death. I thought, *Oh, my God, all hell is death.* Jesus said, "Yes, daughter, but look at the top of the chamber and see what is written." At the top of that chamber, which had the appearance of copper and bronze, there was a huge sign with the words "Trophies of Satan." I said, "Lord, I thought the things in the cages were his trophies." Jesus said, "Behold and look." As I looked into one part of the chamber, Jesus said, "I told you we are in the right arm of hell. The right arm of Satan is very evil, whereas My right arm—as well as the Father's right hand and arm—is very gentle."

[God said,] "*I drew them with gentle cords, with bands of love, and I was to them as those who take the yoke from their neck.*"
(Hosea 11:4)

I saw what looked like a huge python; it was as large as a train and twenty-five to thirty miles in length. This snake was green and yellow with bright colors. And it was alive. At first, it was coiled up, but it uncoiled itself and moved in a circle. Then it curled up into its original position again before uncoiling once more and making a circle. I screamed when I saw large doors open up on the sides of the serpent. I counted twelve of them. Jesus said, "Keep counting." When I got to fifteen, He said, "Wait." There were fifteen open doors, and five more that were shut. Then I saw that there were many rattlers on the snake's tail. I had thought it was a python, but it was actually a rattlesnake.

As I looked at the serpent, Jesus said, "Child, behold and look. Remember that the right arm has power. Remember the right arm; when people shake hands, they shake with the right hand." I saw one door open, and Jesus said, "We are going to go down there, and we are going to look in that door." I said, "Oh, Jesus, what is it?" He said, "What did the sign say? 'Trophies of Satan.'"

Jesus illuminated the area, and the light spread out in a big circle. Behind the rattlesnake were rows and rows of demons holding pitchforks and other things. Many of them also had chains around them and held large keys in their hands. They screamed and ran from the light of the Lord Jesus. The Lord raised His left hand, and fire shot out into the darkness, cremating the demons; they turned into ashes right before my eyes, and smoke arose from their remains. I said, "Oh, Jesus, thank You, thank You." Little snakes were crawling around, but when Jesus pointed toward them, they, too, were cremated.

Jesus said, "My Father gave Me the commandment that I could do this. Child, look, listen, and learn. Things I have shown you and told you, thousands would want to do, but I cannot trust them. Some I can't. Now look."

I saw that where the demons had once been, there was dry, brown ground, with many cracks in it. However, the snake appeared to have grown larger.

Through Door 1

Jesus explained, "We are going to go down there and go through each door. The snake will not be able to do anything." Then the Lord spoke, and we went down a very rocky hill. We walked through the entrance of a large circle called "Trophies of Satan." Door 1 on the side of the serpent was wide open. It was at least ten feet wide and twelve feet high. I thought, *What is this, Lord?* He said, "Look, listen, and learn." (As the Lord recalled this scene to my memory, I remembered that years after He had taken me to hell, while I was praying during a prayer meeting, I had seen a vision of an enormous serpent with doors, similar to what I saw here.)

We walked through the doorway into a large room, and I saw that it contained some very beautiful things. All the rooms we later went into seemed extremely large, though it's hard to estimate their dimensions. This room contained things that Satan had stolen from people to keep them from prospering and to cause them to become discouraged and stop serving God. All around, there were shelves and shelves of beautiful things such as the "rich and famous" would have in their homes—adornments, sheets of beautiful colors, and so on.

I turned around, and Jesus said, "Look above one of these." I saw many gold bars stacked up, so I asked, "What is this?" He said, "Satan's trophies—the money he stole from the church." *Oh, my.* There were stacks and stacks of bars, worth perhaps billions of dollars. Then I looked over at the next shelf, where many books with gold and silver covers were piled up. They seemed to glow. I said, "What is that, Lord?" He replied, "The devil has taken the writings, the truth. He has deceived many in the earth with false teachings, with lies. He has watered down My Word."

The room was like a large warehouse. Jesus showed me all kinds of expensive cars that Satan had stolen. Then He showed me clothing that had been stolen. And accessories. And shoes. All stolen. Jesus stopped in front of the shoes and said, "What do you think these are, Katherine?" "I don't know, Lord, unless You give me the understanding." He said, "These are the 'shoes' of My people, of prophets and apostles, the fivefold ministry. They have stopped walking for Me; they have stopped talking for me. They have laid down and wept; they have given up. Tell My people not to give up but to keep on walking. Don't let their shoes be stolen by Satan. Don't let Satan block them and knock them down. If he does, they must get up and fight him with My Word. I gave My Word to set the captive free."

There were many other shelves. One was full of computers. Another had money floating in it. Jesus said, "This money belongs to My saints. But in My name, it shall be loosed; and in My name, it shall go back up on the earth, and My Father will answer from heaven. Let the people reading this book understand: Do not let the devil take your gifts." Then I began to comprehend about the gifts of the Spirit and how we become lazy when God tells us to do something. We don't want to do it, so we put it off or refuse to do it altogether. Day after day, we procrastinate and don't do what we're meant to do. I've been guilty of that.

See then that you walk circumspectly, not as fools but as wise, redeeming the time, because the days are evil. (Ephesians 5:15–16)

Then Jesus said, "Look in this room." I understood that Satan, the old dragon, had come and seduced us and deceived us. Jesus shook His head and said, "Yes, it is true what you are thinking." I followed Him to another room where there were a large number of swords of the Spirit. The Word was there. It was written on a large sword that was suspended in the air and full of fire.

Jesus said, "In the book of Daniel, it says that My truth was cast down to the ground.[26] The angel Gabriel talked to Daniel,[27] and I sent Gabriel to you, Katherine, a year ago. I sent Him to you, and he gave you some secrets. This is part of the secrets. As I am opening up your mind in remembrance

---

26. See Daniel 8:12.
27. See Daniel 8:15–27; 9:20–27.

of these things, the Angel of Revelation is there with you, and the Holy Spirit."

Then Jesus showed me things that contained the blessings of God for people's bodies. Satan had stolen them with lies, deception, and seduction. The Lord said, "Yes, there are powerful demons out there. When people are in sin, he seduces them. They love the flesh; they love to please it. They do the things they should not do because evil is in them. Evil is in their hearts and their minds, and they need to repent and turn to Me, the Lord Jesus Christ. Child, this room is very, very important, and I will bring you back to it later because there are more things I want to show you here."

While I was recording the revelations for this book, the Lord asked me, "Do you remember the demons that were standing in the circular area? I destroyed them because they were 'strong men,'[28] strongholds upon these things. Tell the people that the greatest weapons are My Word, Jesus Christ's mighty name, the Holy Spirit, the fire of God, the presence of God, and the anointing of God. Awake, church, awake. Awaken the giant that is asleep in the earth."

Through Door 2

As I wrote earlier, there were fifteen open doors in the sides of the snake, and inside each door was something the devil had stolen from the earth. We were finished looking at the room connected with Door 1, and I walked with Jesus through the opening of Door 2. We entered a massive area, at least two hundred miles around. I don't understand it all, but it contained piles of all types of money, neatly stacked. I believe it represented money from the beginning of time until

28. See Matthew 12:29; Mark 3:27; Luke 11:21–22.

now. There were various currencies from all over the earth, and above the money from each nation something was written that I did not understand. I thought, *Oh, my God, this is the money Satan and his demons have stolen from the earth.* "Yes," said Jesus, "and they want to build their own kingdom. They are trying so hard through all kinds of deceitful tricks to rule the nations and take the money. But this day, I destroy it, child; I destroy their plans. I destroy these evil powers by My fire. This fire will not hurt humans, but it truly will break the chains off the humans. And this Holy Spirit fire, the fire of truth and righteousness, has so much power in it. It is alive, because remember that on the day of Pentecost, when the fire came, it sat on the heads of the disciples like cloven tongues. It was alive; you could touch it. Awake, church, and read about My fire; study about My consuming fire. Use My Word!"

Therefore, since we are receiving a kingdom which cannot be shaken, let us have grace, by which we may serve God acceptably with reverence and godly fear. For our God is a consuming fire. (Hebrews 12:28–29)

I watched, listened, and learned. "Exactly what does this money of every nation mean?" I asked. Jesus replied, "When My Father threw the enemy out of heaven, and all of his angels with him that are in everlasting chains and in the middle of hell here, he started thinking of ways to destroy God's people and get back at God. It is war, My daughter, war against good and evil. And I—Jesus Christ, the Son of God, Emmanuel, Yeshua, and other names I have—was the Key. I was the Key and the secret that God was using to bring back hope to the people, to bring back life to My Word."

Big tears flowed from Jesus' eyes, and He said, "Yes, My Word says I'll prosper My people. My Word says that I will give them nations to save. My Word says I will bless them like I did Abraham, like I did Jacob, like I did David. I hope the world understands what I am trying to say. It is a time to be holy. It is a time to get the junk out of your heart and your mind and your soul and your spirit. My Word says, 'Love the Lord thy God with all thy heart and thy mind and thy soul and thy strength.'[29]

"For some of this money, the devil tricked people deceitfully. They were My people, saved and serving Me, but he brought such seducing greed to them. He seduced them with greed to lie, to cheat, to steal with the gifts of God. This goes along with the book of Corinthians."

I stood in awe as I listened to my King explain Door 2. "Children have no food and are dying. Many older people and young people do not have enough money to pay their bills, their rent or anything, so they turn to evil. But I say that as they speak My Word, prosperity will return. Blessings upon blessings I want to give to My people. Tell the earth to repent, and awaken the giant. Tell the earth to repent, My daughter; you blow the trumpet in Zion. Tell My people of their transgressions. Tell My people of their sins."

As we were leaving the room where all the money was, Jesus said, "I want to restore that to My people."

[Jesus said,] *"Therefore do not worry, saying, 'What shall we eat?' or 'What shall we*

29. See, for example, Deuteronomy 6:5 (KJV); Mark 12:30 (KJV).

drink?' or 'What shall we wear?' For after all these things the Gentiles seek. For your heavenly Father knows that you need all these things. But seek first the kingdom of God and His righteousness, and all these things shall be added to you."   (Matthew 6:31–33)

Wake Up and Seek God

We have to hear what Jesus is saying. We must believe Him and arise. There are times when I go through many battles, but I hang on to God's Word. I have seen His Word in action. Many times, when I am praying, I see angels open up a large book, the holy Word of God, and they slam it into the face of that serpent, that dragon, and into his demons, so that they fall and then run. The Word is a wall of protection. Additionally, Jesus gave us His blood and His name as our protection. He is Lord of All.

Let us wake up and seek God. Let us read and understand His Word. It's time for the army of God to arise. He is the living God. He is not made of stone or wood. (See, for example, Daniel 5:23.) Jesus Christ gave His life for you and me so that we could receive eternal life and be with Him forever. Hear ye the Word of the Lord, for Jesus Christ is Lord of All.

Reclaiming the Keys and Gifts of God:

God wants to restore financial provision and other blessings to His people, but we must make sure that our priorities are right and that we are obeying God's Word. Is there a specific sin or transgression that you need to repent of? If so, turn from it and ask God to forgive you. Are you using some of your current resources to help those less fortunate than you are? If not, begin to do what you can to help those in need.

11

Blow the Trumpet in Zion

Through Door 3

Jesus and I had entered Doors 1 and 2 in the side of the serpent, and we next entered Door 3. Immediately, I smelled a very strong stench, and I began to grieve and cry. Tears ran from Jesus' eyes, too. Then He illuminated the place, and I saw stacks and stacks of little coffins. These were the caskets of babies that had died by the trickery of Satan. There also was a table of blood—an abortionist's table, Jesus told me.

I saw something like a timeline, with years and dates flashing in the air in a circle. The dates went back in time very quickly. I also heard the wailing of newborns, and I said, "Father, this is so horrifying." Jesus replied, "Yes, child, this is truly horrible. Satan has stolen many lives. These are his trophies. He keeps a record; he tries to copy God. Satan had these thousands of little boxes and thousands of little coffins put in here as symbols of what he has done. But the babies themselves are not here in hell. Look at them closely; there is no vapor or smoke inside their little bodies." Sure enough, there were no souls inside the tiny skeletons that were in the boxes and coffins.

Jesus emphasized, "I want the world to know that there are absolutely no babies in hell. If someone has told you that there were, what they saw and wrote about was an illusion. It was not the truth."

I thought, *This room is like an illusion of these little babies stacked up here by the thousands and thousands without number.* And the number of caskets seemed to expand. I began to think these truly were Satan's trophies, for which he had seduced and deceived people. Jesus told me, "Yes, this room is an illusion of what Satan has done to the unborn and to the newborn. It is an illusion."

Then Jesus spoke, and everything within Door 3 disappeared for a moment before reappearing. He said, "I want the world to understand that Satan has done this thing. That is why I am showing you this room within this serpent. I am trying to tell the earth all these things and to warn them of Satan's seducing powers. Love Me, trust Me. I want to bring back hope to you. All through hell, people who did these wicked things are burning and screaming. Many people had abortions and never repented, and they are burning in hell here tonight. Please, earth, awake; awake."

I looked all around at the innumerable coffins. The Lord said, "This is a revelation of God to tell the world that from the time of conception, a baby has an eternal soul that is precious to God; that soul is alive. And if you deliberately, willfully abort that child, it is a great sin; it is the sin of murder. You must understand that this sin carries the judgment of God. The blood of aborted babies is crying out to Him from the ground."[30]

For You formed my inward parts; You covered me in my mother's womb. I will praise

30. Genesis 4:8–10.

You, for I am fearfully and wonderfully made; marvelous are Your works, and that my soul knows very well. My frame was not hidden from You, when I was made in secret, and skillfully wrought in the lowest parts of the earth. Your eyes saw my substance, being yet unformed. And in Your book they all were written, the days fashioned for me, when as yet there were none of them.

(Psalm 139:13–16)

Jesus said, "If it is a matter of life or death for the mother, then that is her choice. Yet Satan has tricked many people into thinking that their best option is to get rid of their unborn baby because they won't be able to take care of the child, or they won't be able to give the child a good life, or the child will be an interruption to their own lives. They are being deceived.

"All these little children who were killed are in heaven. God has completed them, and now they are whole. They were meant to bring blessings to people, but instead the people killed them. Oh, the strong force of temptation, the strong force of delusion, when a woman is out there working and tired and single, and she falls in love with a man, and they have that relationship of what they call love. And she ends up pregnant, but he doesn't want the baby and neither does she, and so they go and have it aborted. Over and over, this happens throughout the whole earth. I want young girls to hear Me. Do not have an abortion. I will make a way for you and your baby. Hear what the Spirit of the Lord is saying to the world. Hear, hear, awake!

"If you have had an abortion, and you repent, God will forgive you. Call on Me and ask Me to wash you clean in My blood. I will do it."

We need to bring the teaching of God's Word to young women who are considering having an abortion. If this is your situation, Jesus wants to bring you hope. He does not want you to hurt yourself or your unborn child. Read the Word of God. God is holy. He is pure. He loves you, and He will make a way for you. He will forgive you if you have had an abortion. He is full of grace and mercy.

The LORD is gracious and full of compassion, slow to anger and great in mercy. The LORD is good to all, and His tender mercies are over all His works. (Psalm 145:8–9)

Through Door 4

We left that place and went over to Door 4. I wondered what I would see within that opening because Jesus was crying again. The walls inside were like a large movie screen, depicting the evil things that Satan had done from the beginning of time up until the present. It was like a rotating mural. It showed, for example, demons tormenting people with alcohol and drugs. But then it portrayed the angels of God coming to set them free; many of the people were delivered, and demons were destroyed. Jesus said, "Satan tries to copy God, but he is evil. I come to give life and to give it to you more abundantly. Satan comes to steal, kill, and destroy."[31]

It seemed as if we stood for hours watching these images of the many evil things that had happened over the years, including the Holocaust and various wars. Jesus said, "My daughter, I came to bring peace on the earth, but in the last few years, they have watered down My gospel, so that people don't have the strength to fight or the strength to stand. Many people are being saved in this hour; yes, they are. But knowledge is increasing in the land."

***

[The angel said to the prophet Daniel,] *"At that time Michael shall stand up, the great prince who stands watch over the sons of your people; and there shall be a time of trouble, such as never was since there was a nation, even to that time. And at that time your people shall be delivered, every one who is found written in the book. And many of those who sleep in the dust of the earth shall awake, some to everlasting life, some to shame and everlasting contempt. Those who are wise shall shine like the brightness of the firmament, and those who turn many to righteousness like the stars forever and ever. But you, Daniel, shut up the words, and seal the book until the time of the end; many shall run to*

---

31. See John 10:10.

and fro, and knowledge shall increase."
(Daniel 12:1–4)

I watched many wicked events on the walls of that room. I saw Satan on his throne, laughing about how he had killed thousands of people with earthquakes. And Jesus said, "My covenant is standing for My people. Even if they fall, I send angels to draw them back, and I do it by My Spirit. I send them, My daughter, so that Satan must be bound. I send My powerful Word. Look, I can see many angels fighting for the saints of God and for children." It was so beautiful to watch the glory come in and the blood of Jesus appear. And Satan would be so angry.

The Holocaust was horrifying. As I witnessed those scenes, I screamed, "Oh, God." Tears were coming down Jesus' face, and He said, "My daughter, this also is a vision in hell for you to understand that there are murderers, rapists, and all kinds of evil people in this earth. I want My people to repent, and such things will fall away." Then I saw a scene in which shackles fell off of people. They had been bound, but the chains just melted off.

But I saw other unthinkable horrors, and I thought, *Oh, God, this is awful. I can't stand any more.* Jesus turned to me and said, "You must. You must see these things to tell the people of the earth, to warn them that I love them, that I've sent My power and My presence, that I want them to give all to Me—not just part of themselves, but all to Me—so that they'll have the anointing and the power to set their families free." And then I saw a scene of a crying mother and her babies, and the power of God came and washed and cleansed them with the blood of Jesus. Life came upon them, and they began to receive provision and other good things.

I understood that we must give everything to Jesus. Yes, we are still going to have problems; we must recognize that. But Jesus is trying to tell us, "Return, return to God, you backslider; return to the King of Kings and Lord and Lords. Stop your greed and your unfaithfulness; stop the murderers and the rapists." I fell down and cried. Jesus gently picked me up and said, "Blow that trumpet, My daughter; blow it hard with My love."

We Have Authority over Satan in Jesus' Name

In chapter 14, we will return to the open doors on the sides of the serpent and see the trophies of Satan in the rooms connected with Doors 5, 6, and 7. The "trophies" behind all these doors in the sides of the serpent represent the wickedness that the devil has worked on the earth to stop Christians from arising as a great army to defeat him. Satan has abused us with powerful seductions, but we must understand that we have the authority in Jesus' name to rebuke him. Jesus is truly Lord of All. The Father has given Him all power in heaven, on earth, and below the earth. (See Matthew 28:18.)

Reclaiming the Keys and Gifts of God:

Jesus wants us to give everything to Him—our heart, our soul, our mind, our strength—every aspect of our lives. When we surrender all to Jesus and are continually seeking His purposes, we can live according to His power and anointing. Then we will be able to release our family members and others from Satan's grasp. Have you given all to Jesus? What might you be holding back from Him?

12

Satan's Seducement of the Church

"A Protection to My People"

In this chapter, I want to talk more about hell's punishment and how Satan has seduced people to fall away from God. One time, Jesus and I were walking in hell when the Lord raised His arm in the darkness, as He had so many times before, so that our surroundings could be clearly viewed. I stood in amazement as I looked around. We were in a place where there were thousands and thousands of skeletons stacked up from the ground. They were screaming, "Help us; help us." I looked at Jesus and said, "What is this?" He answered, "These are those who laid down and died for the devil. They gave their hearts and souls to the devil." I said, "Oh, my God. Oh, my Jesus."

I stared at those numberless souls. They were surrounded by laughing demons that were about three feet high. Jesus raised His arm, fire came out, and all those demons were reduced to ashes. The Lord said in regard to the skeletons,

125

"Many people are in the occult and witchcraft and all types of worship of the devil. This is their end if they do not repent. I am calling them to repent today. Repent ye and turn to Me."

One of the corpses screamed, "I was a great voodoo man, and I deceived and killed many and worked many spells on people. But when I died and came here, Satan laughed and said, "This is your kingdom." And all of the skeletons said, "Oh, woe unto us. Why did we do the evil? We were so evil." Then I heard one of the skeletons swear and blaspheme.

I cried for a long time, although without tears. But tears were rolling down Jesus' face. He said, "Humanity, humanity repent. Repent ye, repent. Repent of your evil, your voodoo, your black magic against the innocent, for I will be a protection to My people and a glory in their midst. And My glory will return to the earth.[32] Turn from your evil, you wicked people doing witchcraft and voodoo. Repent, repent in My name, and I will save you. Whosoever calls upon the Lord, I will save them."[33]

If you confess with your mouth the Lord Jesus and believe in your heart that God has raised Him from the dead, you will be saved. For with the heart one believes unto righteousness, and with the mouth confession is made unto salvation. For the Scripture says, "Whoever believes on Him will not be put to shame." For there is no distinction between

---

32. See Zechariah 2:5.
33. See Joel 2:32; Acts 2:21; Romans 10:13.

> *Jew and Greek, for the same Lord over all*
> *is rich to all who call upon Him. For "who-*
> *ever calls on the name of the LORD shall be*
> *saved."* (Romans 10:9–13)

After seeing those stacked skeletons and hearing what they were saying, I thought, *Oh, my God, this is horrible. I can't take it anymore.* So we left that place, and Jesus brought me back home.

A Panoramic View of Judgment in Hell

The next night, Jesus and I were again walking in hell past burning, screaming souls and laughing demons. We were passing by many things I had seen before, such as pits of raging, boiling fire, and an opening in the earth into which skeletons and black objects were falling. It seemed as if I was seeing a panoramic view of hell. Everywhere I looked, souls were being tormented. Many were clothed in fire. There would be flesh on their skeletons for a little while before it melted off like hot lava and slid down around their feet. Their bones would become dry, and worms would crawl out of them. They would scream, gnash their teeth, and cry because they desperately wanted to get out of hell. All around me, a multitude of voices could be heard cursing, blaspheming, and screaming words that I had heard so often during my sojourns in hell: "Why didn't somebody warn me? Why didn't somebody tell me about hell and give me a chance to repent?"

The voices of the dead seemed to get louder and louder, so I asked Jesus about it, and He said, "I wanted you to hear it. Every race and every nation is here. But," He reemphasized, "there are absolutely no babies or children in hell." Then He said, "Look, listen, and learn."

As I looked at that panoramic view of hell, which appeared to be hundreds of miles wide, I also seemed to be able to see right to where individual souls were being tormented, or right to where individual souls were having judgment brought to them. I thought, *Judgment is being carried out by demons in every imaginable, horrible way to torment these lost souls, because these people have the sensation that they have a physical body, and that God has cast both their body and soul into hell.* (See Matthew 10:28.)

Hell Has Enlarged Itself

Jesus said, "We are going to a place where you will hear voices; the dead talk in hell." When we went to this place, I couldn't see the skeletons, but I could hear them. A man's voice said, "I was a serial killer on the earth." Then he screamed at another skeleton, "What did you do?" The second one said, "I killed babies. And I hear the voices of those babies tormenting me in hell." All at once, I heard screams, and I saw demons come up and transform themselves into the form of little babies that were wailing. Then these fabricated forms would burn up and disappear, and the demons would reappear.

I thought, *My Lord, this is an illusion, isn't it?* Jesus replied, "Yes. The devil wants people to abort their children, to kill people, to murder, to steal, to take drugs and alcohol. Listen to some of their conversations."

I heard another man say, "Well, I was an alcoholic, and my wife kept telling me to repent and go get help, but I wouldn't. I became meaner and meaner toward her and more and more of a drunk until my liver was destroyed. Then I died and came here. I never repented, but I did hear that Jesus was the truth, and I knew the way."

After this, I heard the voice of another man saying, "Yes, I was a drug dealer and an alcoholic. I sold drugs, and I began to take hard drugs and died from an overdose. And here I am today, burning and screaming until the day of the great white throne judgment of God. Oh, how I hurt, and oh, how I burn. And I still have the same thoughts and feelings for drugs that I had on earth. I crave drugs, and the craving never leaves me." Then he screamed, "Help me, help me, God."

Then I heard a man moaning. This man had been a gang leader, and he had died a horrible death by gangs. I heard the voice of another soul screaming, "When will this end? Day and night, I suffer. There is no day here; there is no night here. But I know that there were day and night when I was on the earth. Oh, when will this end?"

A woman's voice said, "I was a prostitute. They paid me good money. When I died, I came here, and I suffer so. Can't somebody help me? Why didn't somebody on the earth tell me of this? I heard a little bit about God, but I was never interested. I am the wicked." I looked at Jesus and said, "These are the voices of the dead that are—the dead talk in hell." He said, "Yes, they do. And some of them are still trying to justify their wickedness. These are the souls of the wicked."

Another voice said, "I had sex with an animal, and I died in sin and came here." Another spoke the language of a different nation, but I understood that he was saying, "I was paid to kill people. I blew up trains and planes, and that is why I am here."

All these voices of the dead were talking about the evil they had committed on the earth. As I saw all that activity and heard all those voices, I thought, *Surely, the world needs to be aware of what is down here, because hell has enlarged itself to hold the souls of the wicked.* (See Isaiah 5:14.) I looked at Jesus, and He knew what I was thinking. The Lord said to me, "Child, blow your trumpet in Zion. Tell My people their transgression, and the house of Jacob their sins."

Cry aloud, spare not; lift up your voice like a trumpet; tell My people their transgression, and the house of Jacob their sins.

(Isaiah 58:1)

Demonic Powers Infiltrating the Church

Then Jesus said, "Come on, I am going to show you something else," and we moved into the next area. Jesus caused light to shine, and He cremated demons by His fire. Any demon that the fire didn't touch screamed and ran away. We came to a large opening, which I think was still in the right arm of hell, and there was such an evil section in it—it was like a pool of quicksand and dung with fire. Demons were coming, and they were leading skeletons by the hundreds with black chains around them. The souls were screaming, "Oh, my God, I didn't know hell was real. I mocked. I was an atheist. I made fun. Oh, my God, this is real; this is real."

Then I saw a demon holding a plaque with names on it. This demon was very big and broad-shouldered, and he had fangs, long dirty nails, and big webbed feet. The demons were laughing and saying, "We seduced them. We seduced them." I was greatly grieved at this sight. The name of a soul was called, and demons unchained it, brought it over to the demon with the plaque, and said, "This is your torment; this is your servant. You served the devil well on earth, but in hell you shall be tormented. Satan shall win against God."

I screamed, "No, Lord, no. What have these done, Lord Jesus? What sin of the flesh have they committed?" Jesus said, "Child, listen to the voices of the dead." There were lines and lines of these skeletons bound together, one after another, in black chains. I heard them saying, "Oh, can we get out of here? Is there any hope? Oh, why did we not listen to the gospel of Jesus Christ? Why did we fight against the King who would have saved us from this place? Woe unto us, for our wound is grievous. Woe unto us." Thousands began to say those words and to cry, while others blasphemed God, even though they were in hell.

The demons told these souls, "No man cares for your soul. This is your torment; this is your judgment." I heard two demons scream, in succession, "O fire, burn brighter; fire burn brighter in this quicksand pit to hold more souls that have been seduced by our king, the devil; and we helped him to deceive these."

Jesus said, "I am going to show you a vision in this midst of this revelation." The vision was of one man who had been brought before the large demon. In the vision, the man was on the earth, and he was a preacher of God's Word. Jesus didn't say anything else; the vision said it all. I saw a fine church. I don't know the name of the preacher or the name of his church. I just saw the inside of a large, beautiful church. There was wonderful singing, and people were praising God.

The demon was enjoying looking at this vision; in fact, he was laughing. Then I saw beings in black robes infiltrate the church. They came in, sat down, and were transformed into what looked like church people; then their black robes came back on them. They were demons, but they seemed to be in the form of men and women. After this, I saw the church invite them to assist in the ministry—to work in the office, to help with the offering, and everything. The Christians were so deceived.

Then there was a time lapse of about five years. The church was almost empty, and there was darkness all over it. I looked outside the church building, and the parking lot was cracked and broken up, and the word *Ichabod* was written over the door. (See 1 Samuel 4:19–21.)

I said, "My God, what is this?" Jesus answered, "The Spirit of the Lord has departed from that church building. When those evil powers came in, in darkness, and the black cloaks turned into people, they came as seducing spirits to seduce that church, to check it out. My people are dying from lack of knowledge.[34] They need to understand that they know the Spirit of God. And when they feel this evil around people, they need to pray. They need to go to their pastor and ask him about it; they are not to be paranoid but to know and understand the Spirit of the living God." I thought back to a time when I had spoken at a particular church that was prospering. I had seen evil powers sitting in the audience, but I didn't understand what they were at that time. God hadn't yet given me the knowledge. But a few years later, that church was gone.

Jesus is telling us that if we don't pray for the protection of our fellow believers and travail for those who need to be saved, there will be few spiritual new births. Satan does not

34. See Hosea 4:6.

want us to intercede like that, because he desires to keep people from coming to a knowledge of the truth in Jesus Christ. Once I was participating in a church prayer meeting in which a woman was earnestly travailing for souls to be saved, and I saw another woman go over and lay a hand on the stomach of the first woman, while speaking in a strange language; this caused the woman's travail to abruptly end. The first woman got up and cried, saying, "You stopped my travail." I knew that the second woman was associated with the devil, and it turned out that she was a practicing witch. Some of Satan's workers are deliberately infiltrating our churches. The devil uses people like that to try to stop our travail to God. We must fight against the enemy so that our prayers can go forth to the Lord for ourselves and for the rest of His people.

[The Lord said,] *"I sought for a man among them who would make a wall, and stand in the gap before Me on behalf of the land, that I should not destroy it; but I found no one."*
(Ezekiel 22:30)

I told Jesus, "Oh, my God, this is horrible." Then Christ said, speaking of the church (all believers throughout the world—men and women, boys and girls), "Arise, O bride; My bride, come out of this filth, come out of this. The bride of Christ, arise."

Exercise Discernment and Understanding

As I watched the vision of the church from which the Spirit of the Lord had departed, the dead in hell began to scream and talk again. I said, "Oh, God, you mean all these standing here in chains are going to be thrown into that quicksand because they were deceived and seduced by the devil and enjoyed it?" He said, "I am God. I will save My elect and My righteous from this place. I know how to give them the power to overcome temptation. You blow your trumpet on them and let them seek My Word. It is time to arise from a dead sleep and hear what the Spirit of the Lord is saying to the churches. Repent, repent."

> *Therefore let him who thinks he stands take heed lest he fall. No temptation has overtaken you except such as is common to man; but God is faithful, who will not allow you to be tempted beyond what you are able, but with the temptation will also make the way of escape, that you may be able to bear it.*
> **(1 Corinthians 10:12–13)**

The Lord continued, "Watch over My flock, you leaders. I have given you the discernment and the understanding. Pray with your wife or your husband. You are not alone. Don't be so deceived, saith the Lord, when you know in your heart things aren't right and somebody is trying to destroy you. Satan is very cunning and very wise. He tricks many people. So understand that I came to give life and love and happiness and joy. Help the poor, feed the little children, do the work of an evangelist, preach My Word. For I have many great churches in the earth, and many great pastors and leaders. They take care of the homeless and the widows."

I said, "Jesus, I am so afraid that I will not relate this just like You want it." He replied, "Child, you have the Holy Spirit, and the Holy Spirit is your Leader and your Teacher, bringing all things to your remembrance."

I looked back at the demon that held the plaque of names and saw him take that skeleton whose church I had seen in the vision and throw him into the boiling hot, raging fire and quicksand. Then my eyes were opened to see further into this place, and there were at least twenty more of those quicksand pits, and twenty more demons and many more skeletons screaming and crying. I said, "Oh, my God." Jesus said, "Come and see."

We walked to another area of quicksand where demons were doing the same thing to a different group of skeletons in chains. These souls were some backslidden leaders who had left their cross behind instead of taking it up and continuing to follow Jesus. Some of them had received a great calling, but they had laid down that calling, saying it was too hard. (I know that fulfilling one's calling does get very hard at times.) And then there were others who had been given musical gifts. It seemed to me that their situation was related to some of the glass cages I had seen with the musical instruments and the music sheets. They had stopped using their gifts, and Satan had stolen those gifts and put bondage after bondage on the people, and they wouldn't trust the Lord.

Jesus said, "I have many who have obeyed Me and kept My charge on the earth. I want the world to know—those to whom I have given calls and blessings and great gifts—that your gifts are very important to the body of Christ. How will the bride arise if you don't use your gifts to set the captives free? I gave you the power in My name to set the captives free. That means to rebuke the devil, cast out evil spirits, heal the sick, raise the dead. Awake, awake, My bride. Katherine, awaken them."

Our time in hell was completed for that night. But as Christ was speaking, I was thinking that what He was saying summed up one of the primary purposes for my journey into hell, which is also the main purpose of this book. It was to show us that as time goes on, some people change; they fall and compromise God's Word, and they ultimately end up in hell. We are being warned not to be careless or unfaithful or hard-hearted so that we will not experience the same fate.

These revelations are for today. God is showing us how people end up in hell because they desire the works of the flesh more than obeying God's commandments.

Reclaiming the Keys and Gifts of God:

After reading the following passage of Scripture, answer these questions: In what ways does this passage describe genuine faith? What are some things that cause us to compromise the Word of God? How can we stay faithful to God's Word?

Therefore lay aside all filthiness and overflow of wickedness, and receive with meekness the implanted word, which is able to save your souls. But be doers of the word, and not hearers only, deceiving yourselves. For if anyone is a hearer of the word and not a doer, he is like a man observing his natural face in a mirror; for he observes himself, goes away, and immediately forgets what kind of man he was. But he who looks into the perfect law of liberty and continues in it, and is not a forgetful hearer but a doer of the work, this one will be blessed in what he does. If anyone among you thinks he is religious, and does not bridle his tongue but deceives his own heart, this one's religion is useless. Pure and undefiled religion before God and the Father is this: to visit orphans and widows in their trouble, and to keep oneself unspotted from the world. (James 1:21–27)

13

Awake, My Bride

The Lord Jesus again appeared to me at night, and we were immediately standing in hell. He was holding my spiritual hand, and my hand felt so warm. I looked up at my King, and He said, "Child, this new book that we are doing is given to you by the Holy Spirit, the Father, and Me. This is the one that will bring back and awaken My bride. This is the one that will bring in many souls all over the earth. My hand is upon you, upon this work, and upon your whole family. All things are going to come into order now." I noticed that Jesus was smiling for the first time in a long while.

He continued, "Child, I know it is very hard on you to walk among the dead and to relate these stories, but these are true revelations given from almighty God. And to those who would try to think it is witchcraft, or those who would try to think it is 'way out there,' I say, 'Study your Bible, understand the mysteries, the revelations, given by God Almighty to My prophets and My prophetesses and My apostles.' This is the hour like no other, and I say, 'Woe to you who touch My child, for she is Mine. And hear the Word of the Lord. This book will awaken thousands in the earth and give them the reality and the understanding of how Satan works to destroy them. But yet there is hope in Me; there are blessings in Me; there is truth in Me. And I will watch over you, your families, and all that belongs to you, and I will add blessings, if you will only believe and call out to Me. Now hear ye the Word of the Lord. It is now time for the earth to awaken. Awake, My bride.'" And with that, we began to walk.

God Will Pour Out His Spirit and Grace in Abundance

This time, it seemed only a very short distance to where we were going. Around me were the cries of the dead, the skeletons reaching up and screaming, and the pits. As we walked, Jesus would speak and cause light to appear. At times, demons that came too near the light and the fire of God would be cremated.

The closer we got to the top of a hill, I wondered if it was the same hill I had been on before. Jesus knew my thoughts, and He said, "No. I want to show you something, child." When we reached the summit, we could see everything that was going on in a certain area in hell. I said, "Jesus, are we still in the right arm of hell?" He said, "Yes. The right hand or arm of My Father or of Me or of individuals means power. Now, as you look down below, I want to show you certain torments in this place and explain that Satan has devised and sent out many powerful spirits, seducing powers, against My elect and against the mighty, mighty, mighty power of God. We need people, Katherine, on the earth. We need people to listen to the Spirit of God and to hear His truth. We need the earth to awaken and know that there is a God Almighty over all gods, over every god; a God Almighty, the Lord. Hear what I am saying."

We sat down on a rock, and Jesus said, "Look, child, and behold. God did not make hell for people but for the devil and his angels,[35] but because sin has run rampant, hell has enlarged itself to hold more lost souls. Satan knows much about the kingdom of God, but he does not know all; neither do the angels. My Father is the One who can speak and cause things to happen. I can speak and cause things to happen. Child, there is much for you to report in this book. I am guarding over it with My mighty angels. My warfaring angels are around your home, watching over you and your families. Now, where sin does abound, My grace does much more abound.[36] My Spirit and My grace are going to be poured out in abundance, and thousands are going to come to Me. I have a network of people whom I am going to use to bring in a great revival."

And it shall come to pass afterward that I will pour out My Spirit on all flesh; your sons and your daughters shall prophesy, your old men shall dream dreams, your young men shall see visions. And also on My menservants and on My maidservants I will pour out My Spirit in those days.   (Joel 2:28–29)

Jesus continued, "Now let us talk about what is around us here. Look over to your left." He was revealing to me things about the earth. I looked over to my left, all the way to the

35. See Matthew 25:41.
36. See Romans 5:20.

bottom of the mountain, which appeared to be miles below us. Naturally, there were no trees but only burned, dry, rotten stuff and burned black rocks. I saw a swiftly flowing river, but it was full of corruption, such as dung and slithering snakes. Skeletons were bobbing up and down in this river. I said, "Oh, my God, what is that?" Jesus said, "Child, that is the River of Death. Many times on the earth, I called those people whom you see screaming in the slime. I worked with them, I ministered to them, I sent others to prophesy to them, but they were stiff-necked and strong-willed and would not humble themselves before Me. When death came, they did not have time to repent. They were people whom My Father wanted to use to awaken My bride and put order in the earth. But the enemy used much seduction and many deceiving powers on them. And yes, they knew the way, they understood the way, but they did not want the narrow way. So, they chose the broad way."[37]

As I looked more closely, it was as if I was standing right by the river. Jesus was standing by the river, too. We had instantly moved from the mountaintop down to the river through Jesus' power. And the skeletons, with their bony hands, could see us.

I looked behind me and saw large, ugly demons. Some of them were twenty feet high, some thirty, and some fifty. They were growling, but they could not come near us because of Jesus' power. And then Jesus and I instantly returned to the top of the mountain. The Lord said, "Tell My people out there, Katherine; blow the trumpet in Zion. Tell them that if I have chosen them and called them to repent and turn unto Me, they are able to do the work for Me in the ministry to save the lost from eternal damnation."

---

37. See Matthew 7:13–14.

Then He said, "Look over to your right." As I looked, I saw something down below the mountain that seemed to be an enormous tree, about a hundred feet high and a hundred feet wide, standing in the middle of an area surrounded by muck, dirt, rocks, and fire.

Very quickly, we were down the mountain again, and we were standing next to that huge tree, which was full of corruption and evil and had a horrible stench, like death. I said, "What is this, Lord Jesus?" He said, "This is Satan's tree of evil." Immediately, the tree changed so that it appeared healthy. It looked like it had good fruit on it. I said, "Oh, my Lord, what does this mean?" He said, "Keep watching." I looked again, and the tree had turned to gold; then it turned to silver, and then it turned back into the corrupt tree that it really was. Jesus said, "I have called My bride to be trees of righteousness.[38] Satan therefore has a tree of evil to corrupt My bride, enticing My people with gold, with silver, and with many corrupt ways."

As I watched the tree of evil, its fruit became full of worms and maggots and fell off the branches. Jesus said, "The fruit that people are bearing is like that. They are not using My Holy Scriptures to be humble, kind, and forgiving, and to keep from greed, lust, and the love of money. Their god is money." As Jesus said that, the tree again turned to gold; there were big gold coins all over it. I thought, *Oh, my God, it is all an illusion, isn't it, Jesus?* He said, "It's an illusion that the devil is using to deceive his bride. The true bride of Christ will awaken and praise Me and thank Me for everything, Katherine, good or bad. The true bride of Christ will

---

38. See Isaiah 61:3.

surrender all to Me. I am their King. I am their powerful King. I can do anything for them."

Now to Him who is able to do exceedingly abundantly above all that we ask or think, according to the power that works in us, to Him be glory in the church by Christ Jesus to all generations, forever and ever.

(Ephesians 3:20–21)

I looked at the tree again, and there were strange, wicked-looking objects on it. They were so wicked I can't even describe them. But the tree seemed to enjoy them; it sprang to life, and all at once its leaves were green. New leaves were growing on it, too, but inside them were demonic faces. I said, "Oh, my Lord, what is this?" He said, "This is the occult, the black arts, the white arts of Satan working with him to corrupt My bride. My bride cannot lust after the world; My people must stop their lust and look to Me, for this is an hour like no other. And these things I am showing you in here will awaken My bride. I tell My people to repent. I tell others to repent."

From the top of the mountain, we walked over to another place where there was a huge bank vault sitting on top of a bunch of corruption and floating in debris. Then I saw demons come and open the vault. They put riches into it—gold, paper money, and coins—and they laughed and said, "We deceived people. We stole their money. We had them make bad investments. We had them lie. Oh, is Satan going to be proud of us!"

They had a list of the works they had done on the earth. The vault closed, but many other demons also came and placed into it treasures they had stolen from people on the earth.

There was a bridge over the foul-smelling debris that the vault was floating in. I looked at the Lord and asked, "Jesus, what is this?" He said, "Awaken My bride, My people; tell them not to put their money into foolish things, into lies and debris. Tell My bride to seek first the kingdom of God, and all these things will be added unto them.[39] Tell My bride to awaken to truth and righteousness and to repent of their sins, to truly repent.

"This vault contains things stolen from My bride, things that I had planned for My bride. People say, 'Well, what about Abraham and Isaac and Jacob? They had abundance.' Yes, and you shall have what you need, and some of you shall have abundance to help and to filter back into the kingdom of God. But, My bride, you have greed in you. You have the spirit of greed and lust. Repent, My bride, of greed and lust."

So are the ways of everyone who is greedy for gain; it takes away the life of its owners.
(Proverbs 1:19)

Pray for the World and Seek God's Counsel

We walked on to another area, and Jesus showed me a vision that amazed me. There was a huge bar, or tavern, that

39. See Matthew 6:33.

looked just like one on the earth. In it, some people were play-ing pool and others were sitting at the bar drinking, but they were so drunk; they were so evil. A man got up and stabbed another man. The man who had been stabbed pulled a gun, but then he dropped dead because somebody else had sud-denly shot him. I screamed, "Oh no, Lord, You said this is going on in the earth today."

Then He showed me a flash of something that I didn't understand. There were scenes upon the earth of great cor-ruption and violence. Jesus said, "Awaken My bride to pray." He showed me little children who were being used for sex objects. It was as if I was watching a movie of various corrupt things going on throughout the whole earth. He said, "Tell My bride to awaken and pray. Tell people to repent of their sins." I said, "Oh, Jesus; oh, Jesus."

He said, "Come, there is much more to show you." We went to an area where there were many huge cages. I wept when I saw them. I was standing beside the Lord, and He was crying, too. Jesus told me, "Child, look at the cages." In each cage was something that was part human and part beast. He said, "Man is trying to copy God and create a hu-man with beasts. They are trying to raise an army. My Father is so grieved over this, and I am so grieved, that He is going to destroy the earth with great judgment if My bride does not awaken and begin to pray and seek His counsel and do what I say. There are secret laboratories all over the earth, including the jail system. Woe to you, earth, woe to those doing this, for they are using the jail inmates for scientific purposes, and you never hear from them again. Woe, saith Jesus, to these evil works in the earth and to those who are operating them."

I began to cry again. Jesus said, "Come and see this, child. Awaken My bride; blow the trumpet in Zion." We went to a different area, and I was shown another vision. Jesus said, "Look and behold." I saw a very large hospital on which the word "Death" was written. Many pregnant women were standing inside. They would go into the abortion room, at least five at a time, and different doctors would abort their babies. I saw the blood flow out of the women and onto the floor. Some of the women died, and the doctors actually killed some of the women and the babies. I said, "Oh, my God, how can this be?" He said, "Secret laboratories. Look at the baby." The baby was part beast and part human.

I remembered that many years ago, I had had a vision of the same thing. I had been deep in prayer when the Lord showed me this, and I've never revealed it until now. Jesus said, "It is time to warn the earth that this wickedness must stop; it is time for My people to arise and seek God for wisdom and knowledge."

The Call of God

Jesus and were back at the top of the mountain, and He said, "There is a time to reap and a time to sow. This book is coming out just on time.

"I have many fine churches in the earth and many fine leaders. But yet I need more to arise and to answer My call and to be chosen by God. After you are called by God, you walk through testing times and times of trial. It's like an army. An army goes through a lot to be on the front lines. God calls you, and then, when you answer, Satan will put you through certain situations, but then God always delivers. He knows how to deliver the godly out of temptation.[40] But I need more people to stop being occupied with the cares of the world and to hear what I am saying. I have chosen you, Katherine, as a prophetess, a visionary, a writer, for you were born to see and to tell these things. And in the midst of it, I blessed you with children, a home, grandchildren, great-grandchildren. I blessed you. And I am going to continue to bless you, little one, for you are sincere and you are righteous in Me. You are a tree of righteousness, and you are bearing good fruit."

As we were sitting on that mountain in hell, I was thinking about how Jesus was talking to me and encouraging me. And all around, I saw thousands who hadn't obeyed Him. I saw thousands and thousands who hadn't understood that hell was real. I began to be grieved again. I held the Lord's hand, and we both wept. He said, "Child, I raised up others, too, to whom I showed hell. And some of them were made to tell about it. Some of them were afraid. Some of them just said, 'Absolutely no; I'll never tell it. They'll think I'm crazy.' Behold, I've told you secret things that you've never told anybody. Behold, there is much more that I am going to reveal to you. But if the people would hear and listen to the Holy Bible and to the voices of the apostles, prophets, evangelists, pastors, and teachers, they would understand that the call of God is so important. And then the enemy comes and sends everything in your way to get you caught up in the cares of the world."

The ones sown among thorns…are the ones who hear the word, and the cares of this world, the deceitfulness of riches, and the

---

40. See 2 Peter 2:9.

> *desires for other things entering in choke the word, and it becomes unfruitful. But these are the ones sown on good ground, those who hear the word, accept it, and bear fruit: some thirtyfold, some sixty, and some a hundred.*
> (Mark 4:18–20)

Often, when I have been in prayer, the Holy Spirit has said, "I called, and I called, and I called. And I call those to repent and to come unto Me. And I call, and I call, and they do not come. They are too busy with the cares of this world to stop and hear what I have to say."

We must make time for God. Yes, we have to take time to address the concerns in our life. We have to take time for our children. We have to take time for other things. But if we put God first, it will all fall into place. Of course, we are going to make mistakes and fall short, but God understands that. He is not going to crush us or destroy us when we fail or make a mistake. He loves us so much. He is concerned about us, our children, our grandchildren, and our great-grandchildren. He cares about all our loved ones. He made a covenant with us when He went to the cross and shed His powerful blood for us. And we have a God who will keep His covenant with us even if we fall. He is there to pick us up, to give us hope, and to tell us how much He loves us and wants us to continue on.

I looked at Jesus my Savior, and His face began to light up. He touched me and gave me strength. Even now, He is touching me and giving me strength. I think back on the call of God for my life. Truly, to be chosen by God is the greatest honor in the world. But if all of you pastors, evangelists, and other fivefold ministry leaders wrote a book about your life, I know it would describe trials and heartaches similar to the ones I've had. It would reveal some of the difficulties that you've walked through but never before told anyone about. It would show how much you love God, and how you rejected the devil when he came and tempted you with fleshly desires, and how you've had to give up many things that the world refers to as pleasures—but that do not bring pleasure to God—because you are accountable to Him. The responsibility of God's leaders, and of all His children, is very serious. I know this book will bring much wisdom and knowledge from God for the body of Christ and for those who need to repent of their sins and receive Jesus as their Lord and Savior.

Thank You, God. I love You and trust You. You are our Father, our Savior, our Healer, and our Deliverer.

Reclaiming the Keys and Gifts of God:

Have you been spending time with God regularly? If not, begin today to set aside time daily to worship God, to pray, to read His Word, and to seek His counsel. Ask Him to show you how to pray for the needs of your loved ones and for the state of the world.

14

Back to the Doors

The next night, when Jesus took me into hell, He said, "Come, child, we are going back to the doors of hell. I told you I would bring you back here." In chapters 10 and 11, I described how we had gone to the "Chamber of Death," where we began to enter the open doors in the sides of the large serpent. Each door represented the wickedness of the devil—something that Satan had taken from the body of Christ through his temptations and deceit and was holding captive, or something that Satan had inflicted on the people of the earth.

Door 1 contained many beautiful, valuable items, and Door 2 had piles of money from nations around the globe. These things had been stolen by Satan to rob God's people of His blessings and to deplete their means of spreading the gospel and helping the poor. Door 3 was the illusion of the coffins from the multitude of babies that had died as a result of Satan's trickery. Door 4 held the "movie theater" depicting many of Satan's evil acts throughout history.

Again, there were fifteen open doors and five closed ones in the snake. In this chapter, I will describe Doors 5 through 7. (An account of the other doors will be given in a later book.)

Through Door 5

As Jesus and I walked through Door 5, I received a word in my mind from Jesus, saying, *The devil has stolen the communication between the people, the communication to Me, the prayers to Me, and the prayers for the people's family members and others. He has stolen the communication that I want from My people.*

Inside Door 5 was a very large room that looked like an office in a corporation or a bank. There were desks, computers, printers, sound devices, and paperwork. I said to Jesus, "What is this, Lord?" He replied, "The devil has stolen the communication between My people and Me, and also from My people's families. Whereas they should be communicating and talking and praying, they are fighting and arguing and doing the things of the world. The devil makes sure that there are times when people do not communicate. He works devices of evil to separate people and to separate things that should not be separated. For instance, when a ministry is going well, and the staff is all there and the leader gives people instructions, some of those people have not yet died to the flesh. They are with Me, but they are still in the world, too. They have not overcome, and I want them to overcome. I want them to stop complaining, murmuring, and grumbling and to seek My counsel and My face for the communication between them and God."

Therefore, my beloved, as you have always obeyed,...work out your own salvation with fear and trembling; for it is God who works in you both to will and to do for His good

pleasure. Do all things without complaining and disputing, that you may become blameless and harmless, children of God without fault in the midst of a crooked and perverse generation, among whom you shine as lights in the world, holding fast the word of life.
(Philippians 2:12–16)

Jesus continued, "It is now time for the world to awaken and for people to recognize where they have hurt or wounded anybody deliberately. I am not saying innocently, but if you have done it deliberately and willfully and with manipulation, you need to repent. You need to come back to holiness, and you need to go make amends with your brother and your sister. Now, there are other times when what happens is justified. But always seek My face, seek My counsel, and obey Me; do what I tell you to do and read My holy Word."

I turned to the Lord and said, "You mean, Lord, even in our own lives, we don't communicate with certain people and clear up certain matters that are important to us because we fear that we are going to hurt or offend them?" And the Lord said, "That is true. I want My people to know that I love them and that there is My grace and My forgiveness. I want them to begin to communicate again and to love again and to share again. And I want to restore the hearts of the fathers to the children and the children's hearts unto the fathers—and that also means restoring people's hearts to God, My Father and your Father. I want to restore your relationships like the spirit of Elijah.[41] I want to restore the relationship between

_____
41. See Malachi 4:6; Luke 1:17.

the people and My God; and in My name, you can restore that. You now have the power in My name to come to God anytime and ask for help from the sanctuary."[42]

I looked at Jesus, and strength came to His face. Of course, strength was already there, but I saw something else reflected, like a new hope. I said, "Lord, it looks like there is hope all over You." And He said, "Yes, yes. These revelations of My Word will awaken My bride and bring back hope to the people, for I am a God who loves and forgives. Have them communicate with Me and talk to Me and tell Me their troubles and their sorrows. I will care because I love them unconditionally. I hate wickedness, I hate evil, but I love My people. And I love the sinners, though not the evil things they are doing. Many of My people used to do the things of the world, but they turned from those things. They made up their minds, and they turned from their wicked ways back unto God. And I helped them overcome. That's My Word. That's My promise. And the Holy Spirit is a Comforter. Come, child, we are going to Doors 6 and 7."

Let us awaken to what Jesus is saying to us! We must be restored to God and to other people whom we have hurt and offended! It is a sin to manipulate and abuse others; this is a manifestation of the lusts of the flesh, "*fulfilling the desires of the flesh and of the mind*" (Ephesians 2:3). Those who do not repent, receive Christ, and remain in the love of God will face consequences for their manipulation. For example, in another place in hell, I had seen an enormous pile of mud that had four sides and reminded me of a skyscraper. Out of the top of it, mud spewed out like an exploding volcano. The thick mass of "mud lava" flowed into the river. Stuck within

---

42. See Psalm 20:2.

that mud were souls who had manipulated people on earth. They were screaming to die because they were being carried by this stream of mud up through the mud tower and out the top of it and down to the river again in an endless cycle.

Let us therefore humble ourselves, go to the Lord, repent of all our sins, and learn to love Him and other people.

Humble yourselves under the mighty hand of God, that He may exalt you in due time, casting all your care upon Him, for He cares for you.　(1 Peter 5:6–7)

Through Door 6

I asked, "Lord, what's in Door 6?" He said, "Awaken My people; let them hear the sound of the alarm." I thought, *What in the world is in Door 6?* Inside, there were puzzles and games everywhere. There were tables with checkerboards and other kinds of games that I had never seen before. Jesus said, "This is called the Game Door, where people play games with God, where people threaten God." I saw writings on the wall in which people were declaring things like, "God, if You don't do this, I'm not going to do that." I heard voices saying, "I blame You, God, for my child dying." Then I heard other voices demanding, "Who do You think You are, God? I am not going to do this." I heard all kinds of excuses, all kinds of judgment of God, in the voices of men and women. I even heard people tell God, "Well, I am going to turn to Satan because he can give me more. I am going to go follow another god. I don't believe You." Such words were coming and going in this room. I told Jesus, "Oh, my Lord, this is horrible, horrible, what the people are saying against God."

Nobody was at the tables with the games, but the puzzle parts would move on their own, as if a force was controlling them. However, nothing about the games would fit or work out. I began, "Lord Jesus—," and then I saw writing appear on tablets. I don't know who was doing the writing, but the words were blaspheming God, blaming God, and saying that they had turned from God to familiar spirits.

I fully understand that these evil works were the result of Satan's efforts to get people to backslide, but the other side of it is that the Holy Spirit would give people a word or a prophecy from God, and many of them would change and return to Him; they would regain their hope and read their Bible.

The lessons from Door 6 are very important. Awake, bride of Christ. You have to stop blaming and hating God when something goes wrong. To do so is a great error. God Almighty could smite and destroy you if He wanted to, but He loves you and cares for you. Stop blaming Him and turn back to Him. He is the One who can help you.

I was very upset when we left Door 6, and I said, "Jesus, what awful, awful things." I looked down the row of other doors that we had not yet gone into, and I thought, *I don't know if I can take this.* However, we continued on.

Through Door 7

We walked through Door 7, and Jesus said, "This is a vision. I am showing a church service." Many people were praising God with their hands raised. Some people were barely raising their hands and praising God, which was okay. And Jesus said, "I read the hearts of people."[43] When the people lowered their hands, I could read their hearts, too. I saw that the hearts of many of them were not clean. Many of them were continuing in their sins. Some people's hearts had black in them and some had white in them.

Then the service was over, and the people left. Some of them got in their cars and began to curse and blaspheme God. I said, "Oh, my Lord, they were in there praising Him." One person went out after church and got stone drunk. Another went out and sat with drug dealers. Other people did other wrong things.

The Lord said, "Yes, many whom I call unto Me have a lot of sin in their hearts, Katherine. And I want them to know I love them, but I want to change them. The ones with a bright light on them that you saw praising Me were those who have overcome. I want My people to overcome the sins of their flesh. I want them to call upon Me and ask Me to help them and deliver them. It is good that they go to My house and learn, even if they have not overcome yet. That is why I am showing you this in hell. This deceitfulness, this covertness, this drawing back to the world is from hell. I come to give My people liberty. I come to give them freedom and love."

Now the Lord is the Spirit; and where the Spirit of the Lord is, there is liberty. But we all, with unveiled face, beholding as in a mirror the glory of the Lord, are being transformed into the same image from glory to

43. See, for example, 1 Chronicles 28:9.

glory, just as by the Spirit of the Lord.
(2 Corinthians 3:17–18)

Then Jesus said, "Now I want to show you another church service." The first vision went away, and I thanked God for His grace that pulls us in even when we haven't yet overcome. In the next vision, there was a wonderful movement of the power of God. I don't know where the church service was, but the people were shouting and praising, and all their hearts, except perhaps those of a few in the back of the church, were aflame for God.

Jesus said, "Katherine, bring liberty to My people through this book. Bring liberty back to My people." Then He shouted, "Liberty. Where God is, there is liberty!"

Lord, that is awesome, wonderful, beautiful!

Reclaiming the Keys and Gifts of God:

When things go wrong in your life, how do you react? Do you tend to blame God for them? Or do you keep trusting Him and thanking Him in the midst of the situation? When we blame God, we open the door for Satan to draw us away from our heavenly Father and His truth. God loves us unconditionally and cares for us. If you have been blaming God for anything, tell Him how you feel about what has gone wrong. Ask Him to forgive you for holding this situation against Him. Then ask Him to use it for good in your life, as only He is able to do, so that He can restore your joy and spiritual strength.

And we know that all things work together for good to those who love God, to those who are the called according to His purpose. (Romans 8:28)

15

Prepare the Way of the Lord

I t's been almost forty years since God first gave me revelations of hell. As I related things in this book that I've never before told anyone or written down, it was as if I was reliving it. Sometimes it feels as if all these things that Jesus reveals to me are too much, but He does so for the sake of people in every nation of the world. He wants them to know God, to live a life of freedom in Him, and to be saved for eternity.

Jesus Will Show Himself Strong

Jesus has revealed to me more sections of hell in the last few years. For example, He showed me where there was a big sign in hell that said "False Gods." In that place, millions of souls were burning; fire came over their heads and under their feet; the fire flowed, then came together in a narrow space and burst out and shot up, falling down a mountainside that was burned and dry. As the screams of souls filled the air, Satan laughed and roared in the background. I thought, *Oh my God, who's going to stop people from reaching these fires?*

I remember looking up and seeing a dark opening. Jesus caused light to shine, and I could see many more skeletons falling down into the fire. Then He said, "Come on, I want to show you another thing." I said, "What is it, Lord?" He replied, "I know the heart of every man and woman, and when they give their heart to me, I come to live inside of them and be with them; I teach them and guide them. But I also know that there are many people with wicked hearts who can't wait to hurt, kill, steal, or lie, and yet I send workers to them. I send My Word to them to repent; I give them a space to repent. I send out My great mercy and grace.

"As you notice, there are many worms teething on these bones of the skeletons, and they feel that, Katherine. It's excruciating pain, and there's no relief." I thought, *Oh, God, thank You for saving me; thank You for saving people whom I know. Thank You, Jesus, for coming to earth to be our Savior.* And Jesus said, "My daughter, as I told you before, I'm going to raise up others who have seen hell. But I'm going to raise up some new people to see hell as the movie about this book is being made. I'm going to prove to the world who I am. And I'm going to do things and show Myself strong in these last days."

Evil Will Be Uncovered

As we walked, multitudes and multitudes were burning. Thousands of voices were clanging, "Let us die; let us die." I knew that many of these souls had come there since Jesus had first shown me hell. I *knew* it. And Jesus said, "Yes, child, I'm revealing to you new things, things that are so sad and so powerful that some people will be saved from the very fires of hell because of what I'm showing you."

It is so, so sad to understand this wisdom of God. Oh, how horrible to be in hell.

Jesus continued, "There are many seducing spirits in the earth, and yes, I did open your mind, bring back your remembrance to know all these things you've been talking about. But these are some new things now that I'm showing you and telling you. In heaven, God has a justice scale, just like any courtroom on the earth. My Father is a righteous Judge, He's a holy Judge, and you're going to see a place here for lawyers, doctors, and thieves who lied in the courtrooms, even some judges who lied for that 'almighty dollar,' the money. There are some righteous lawyers, judges, and doctors who deal justly with people. I am not talking about them."

I looked into that place and saw thousands of men and women who were wearing beautiful suits or other professional clothes. And then I saw the earth shake underneath them, and fire burst up out of the earth and engulfed them. Their clothes burned off, and they melted down to skeletons who screamed, "Let us die!" Jesus said, "My Word says, 'Woe to the lawyers.'[44] They have put many innocent people in jail, My child. They've let the wicked go free. They have put men and women in prison who did not need to be there. They have done many wicked things. If you notice, there were jail keepers in there also. They did it for the 'almighty dollar' and 'almighty manna.' I've seen people being beaten and killed, and then buried or burned—destroyed—in these prisons and jails in the earth, as if nobody knew. But I know. My Father knows. And a lot of this is going to be uncovered. When God sends His Spirit to uncover it, watch out, world!"

Again, there are honest lawyers, judges, and prison guards who deal justly with people. But there are others who commit terrible things such as these.

---

44. See Luke 11:46, 52.

I cringed as we walked away from that sight. Once more, I heard Jesus say, "Woe to the lawyers." And I thought, *These Scriptures are being fulfilled.*

The Lord Jesus turned to me, looked into my eyes, and said, "Child, we're going to go now. And this is the end of the journey for a while. I love you so much, and I'll be with you in the days ahead. I'll help you. I'll be with your family. I love you, child."

Then I heard Him say, "I'm coming to talk to you tomorrow night." With that, I was back in my home.

Satan's Vision Is Corrupt

The next night, Jesus came and took me into hell one more time. The Lord said, "We're going to go to the eyes of hell, child." We went in where there were hollowed-out holes; all around them, as well as down into the head of hell, there were things that looked like rocks. And I saw the jaws of hell open and demons laughing.

I asked, "Lord, what are we doing here?" He said, "Look, listen, and learn." I watched as the circle around the eyes began to fill with worms and maggots. Satan came, and he had some kind of bucket. He scooped burning stuff into it and gave it to the demons to pour on the burning skeletons. Again, the fire didn't burn the worms or the rest of the vile stuff—just the skeletons. And Satan was laughing.

I looked at Christ, and He was crying. He said to me, "Child, you're going to tell the world about this place. And a movie shall be made out of this book. The world shall know that I am God Almighty. Bible Scriptures will come alive to people. They will fear the judgment of thy Father and turn unto Him. My Father and your Father gave Me permission to bring you here and to show you these things to prepare the earth for My return. I don't know when I will return; only My Father knows, not even the angels.[45] But I say to you, "Prepare ye the way of the Lord."

As it is written in the book of the words of Isaiah the prophet, saying: "The voice of one crying in the wilderness: 'Prepare the way of the LORD; make His paths straight. Every valley shall be filled and every mountain and hill brought low; the crooked places shall be made straight and the rough ways smooth; and all flesh shall see the salvation of God.'"

(Luke 3:4–6)

Then Jesus said, "Let's go." We began to ascend out of that place and into the fresh air above. I was so grateful. Yet, as we left, I could still hear the cries of the multitudes, the gnashing of teeth, the regret, the sorrow. I felt so sad and helpless. After we arrived at my home, Jesus sat by my bed until daylight, saying to me, "Peace, be still."

Believe in Jesus Christ

Jesus is so tender, so precious. I am telling you these things that He has related to me because He has asked me to, and because He loves you. Jesus doesn't want you to go to hell. He wants you to repent while you still can. He doesn't

---

45. See Matthew 24:36.

want you to think you have lots of time left on earth and then suddenly die and be gone from this life, only to end up in hell. Repent and trust in the Lord. Live for Him. Start attending a good church. Tell the truth about heaven and hell to your family members and neighbors, and let the Spirit of God draw them to salvation. Love one another as Christ has loved you. (See, for example, John 13:34.)

Hell is a place we need to fear so that we will not become complacent about our lives. We need to fear the judgment of God. We should fear God not because He can destroy us but because we reverence and love Him. We need to keep His Word as best we can. And if we fall, we must repent right away. Let us repent of all our sins and recommit our lives to God.

I don't really care if critics or other people laugh at this account, because I know a God who is going to show you that He is real. You don't want to die and wake up in hell for eternity because you didn't believe in Him. You can be saved. God asks you to believe that His Son Jesus Christ came to earth to die on the cross for your sins. He asks you to repent of your sins and to receive Jesus' sacrifice on your behalf, so that you can be cleansed from those sins through Jesus' precious blood.

If you don't know Jesus as your Savior, I urge you to receive Him right now. You can do so by praying this prayer:

Heavenly Father,

I believe in You and in Your Son Jesus Christ, who came to earth to die on the cross for my sins. I believe that You raised Him from the dead and that He is alive forever, so that everyone who believes in Him can receive eternal life. Because of what Jesus did for me, I ask You to forgive all my sins and to come into my heart and save my soul. Fill me with Your Holy Spirit, and help me to live for You from this day forward. Thank You for saving me and giving me a new life. In Jesus' name, amen.

For whatever is born of God overcomes the world. And this is the victory that has overcome the world—our faith. Who is he who overcomes the world, but he who believes that Jesus is the Son of God? (1 John 5:4–5)

Stand in Freedom

If you already know Jesus Christ, remember that He came to set us free. The Lord told me, "Bring liberty to My people through this book." And the Scriptures say, "*It is for freedom that Christ has set us free. Stand firm, then, and do not let yourselves be burdened again by a yoke of slavery*" (Galatians 5:1 NIV).

We can live in freedom when we love God and stay faithful to Him, and when we recognize and expose Satan's deceptions. The Lord is calling all Christians to repent, to give ourselves wholeheartedly to Him, to understand the reality of hell, and to fight spiritually for those who are lost, sick, and oppressed by the devil. We need to exercise the gifts of the Spirit that God has given to us. And we must study the keys to the kingdom and diligently use them to win back what Satan has stolen from us.

In this book, we have discussed many keys to the kingdom, such as:

+ binding and loosing
+ the name of Jesus
+ obedience to God
+ compassion
+ love
+ a humble spirit
+ spiritual discernment
+ praise
+ prayer
+ righteousness
+ the true Word of God
+ faith
+ the fire of God
+ the gifts of the Spirit
+ the restoration of the fivefold ministry gifts

When we all repent of our sins, when we turn to Jesus wholeheartedly, when we reject worldliness, disobedience, laziness, and greed, and when we use the keys to the kingdom and the gifts that Jesus has given to us, we can defeat Satan and reclaim the blessings and provision of God that we allowed the enemy to take from us. Remember that Jesus said this is a time of judgment for many of Satan's demons, when they will be destroyed and turned to ashes. This is a time for binding and loosing. We can have victory over the devil, and we can bring many people into salvation, freedom, and prosperity in God. We can bring deliverance, turning people from the power of Satan unto God, in Jesus' name! (See Acts 26:18.)

I recommend that you read this work alongside your Bible and balance what is written here with the Holy Scriptures. Love Jesus with all your heart, and serve Him to the glory of God!

Remember, if you fail and feel like giving up, go back to Jesus. He will be there to lift you up. Turn to Him for help, for He has promised to take you back. (See, for example, John 6:37.)

Receive Everlasting Life

Just as I was finishing *A Divine Revelation of Satan's Deceptions*, the Lord gave me a vision to share with you so that you would understand His intention for this book. I saw the hands of the Lord, and light was upon them. In His left hand, the Lord was holding an old-fashioned, long-necked, transparent bottle. With His right hand, He began to unscrew the lid. The water inside that bottle was alive!

And the Lord told me that you should read about His *"living water"* in John 4:10–14, 23 and John 7:38. The reason for this entire book is to pour out His living water on us. He also said to read about the *"bread of life"* in John 6:35–58. He wants to bring us into an understanding of who He is and of the bread of life He wants to give us, if we would only come to Him. This living water, this bread of life, is everlasting life. When we receive Christ, we have life eternal with Him, and we will never die.

For God so loved the world that He gave His only begotten Son, that whoever believes in Him should not perish but have everlasting life. (John 3:16)

EPILOGUE

Words of Liberty from the Lord

The spirit of prophecy (see Revelation 19:10) spoke to me and said, "Yea, saith the Spirit of the Lord, this is the end of this book, but there will be another book to reveal more to the body of Christ. This book will bring liberty, liberty, liberty to My people and to sinners. I will bless this book. It will go around the world in every language. This book, My daughter, will be blessed financially. This book is of God Almighty. It is dedicated to the Father, to the Son, and to the Holy Spirit. It is liberty I am bringing through these pages, My children. Arise, My bride. Awake, My bride. Awake, My preachers and My leaders. Come back to Me, for I love you. And I need you. I need you in the earth to spread My gospel; I need you for the work of God. The supernatural power of God will come and give you visions and dreams and revelations. So, this is the work of the Holy Spirit, My children. And yea, I say that liberty will come through the reading of this book and of the Holy Bible. Liberty, My children; this is to all, saith the Lord Jesus Christ."

Select Scriptures on Satan, Spiritual Deception, and Temptation

Satan's Characteristics

The devil...was a murderer from the beginning, and does not stand in the truth, because there is no truth in him. When he speaks a lie, he speaks from his own resources, for he is a liar and the father of it.

(John 8:44)

The thief [the devil] does not come except to steal, and to kill, and to destroy. (John 10:10)

He who sins is of the devil, for the devil has sinned from the beginning. For this purpose the Son of God was manifested, that He might destroy the works of the devil.

(1 John 3:8)

Be sober, be vigilant; because your adversary the devil walks about like a roaring lion, seeking whom he may devour. (1 Peter 5:8)

The great dragon was cast out, that serpent of old, called the Devil and Satan, who deceives the whole world; he was cast to the earth, and his angels were cast out with him. Then I heard a loud voice saying in heaven, "Now salvation, and strength, and the kingdom of our God, and the power of His Christ have come, for the accuser of our brethren, who accused them before our God day and night, has been cast down." (Revelation 12:9–10)

Satan's Deceptions

The LORD God said to the woman, "What is this you have done?" The woman said, "The serpent deceived me, and I ate." (Genesis 3:13)

For false christs and false prophets will rise and show great signs and wonders to deceive, if possible, even the elect. (Matthew 24:24)

If our gospel is veiled, it is veiled to those who are perishing, whose minds the god of this age has blinded, who do not believe, lest the light of the gospel of the glory of Christ, who is the image of God, should shine on them. (2 Corinthians 4:3–4)

The coming of the lawless one is according to the working of Satan, with all power, signs, and lying wonders, and with all unrighteous deception among those who perish, because they did not receive the love of the truth, that they might be saved. And for this reason God will send them strong delusion, that they should believe the lie, that they all may be condemned who did not believe the truth but had pleasure in unrighteousness.

(2 Thessalonians 2:9–12)

Then I saw an angel coming down from heaven, having the key to the bottomless pit and a great chain in his hand. He laid hold of the dragon, that serpent of old, who is the Devil and Satan, and bound him for a thousand years; and he cast him into the bottomless pit, and shut him up, and set a seal on him, so that he should deceive the nations no more till the thousand years were finished. But after these things he must be released for a little while. (Revelation 20:1–3)

Satan's Temptations

Then Jesus was led up by the Spirit into the wilderness to be tempted by the devil. And when He had fasted forty days and forty nights, afterward He was hungry. Now when the tempter came to Him, he said, "If You are the Son of God, command that these stones become bread." But He answered and said, "It is written, 'Man shall not live by bread alone, but by every word that proceeds from the mouth of God.'" Then the devil took Him up into the holy city, set Him on the pinnacle of the temple, and said to Him, "If You are the Son of God, throw Yourself down. For it is written: 'He shall give His angels charge over you,' and, 'In their hands they shall bear you up, Lest you dash your foot against a stone.'" Jesus said to him, "It is written again, 'You shall not tempt the LORD your God.'" Again, the devil took Him up on an exceedingly high mountain, and showed Him all the kingdoms of the world and their glory. And he said to Him, "All these things I will give You if You will fall down and worship me." Then Jesus said to him, "Away with you, Satan! For it is written, 'You shall worship the LORD your God, and Him only you shall serve.'" Then the devil left Him, and behold, angels came and ministered to Him.   (Matthew 4:1–11)

Watch and pray, lest you enter into temptation. The spirit indeed is willing, but the flesh is weak.
                                             (Matthew 26:41)

Therefore let him who thinks he stands take heed lest he fall. No temptation has overtaken you except such as is common to man; but God is faithful, who will not allow you to be tempted beyond what you are able, but with the temptation will also make the way of escape, that you may be able to bear it.   (1 Corinthians 10:12–13)

Let the husband render to his wife the affection due her, and likewise also the wife to her husband. The wife does not have authority over her own body, but the husband does. And likewise the husband does not have authority over his own body, but the wife does. Do not deprive one another except with consent for a time, that you may give yourselves to fasting and prayer; and come together again so that Satan does not tempt you because of your lack of self-control.   (1 Corinthians 7:3–5)

Blessed is the man who endures temptation; for when he has been approved, he will receive the crown of life which the Lord has promised to those who love Him. Let no one say when he is tempted, "I am tempted by God"; for God cannot be tempted by evil, nor does He Himself tempt anyone. But each one is tempted when he is drawn away by his own desires and enticed. Then, when desire has conceived, it gives birth to sin; and sin, when it is full-grown, brings forth death. (James 1:12–15)

Satan's Distortion of God's Word/False Doctrine

Now the Spirit expressly says that in latter times some will depart from the faith, giving heed to deceiving spirits and doctrines of demons, speaking lies in hypocrisy, having their own conscience seared with a hot iron...."
(1 Timothy 4:1–2)

For such are false apostles, deceitful workers, transforming themselves into apostles of Christ. And no wonder! For Satan himself transforms himself into an angel of light. Therefore it is no great thing if his ministers also transform themselves into ministers of righteousness, whose end will be according to their works.
(2 Corinthians 11:13–15)

A servant of the Lord must not quarrel but be gentle to all, able to teach, patient, in humility correcting those who are in opposition, if God perhaps will grant them repentance, so that they may know the truth, and that

they may come to their senses and escape the snare of the devil, having been taken captive by him to do his will.
(2 Timothy 2:24–26)

Satan's Stealing of the Word/Trials/ The Cares of the World

The sower sows the word. And these are the ones by the wayside where the word is sown. When they hear, Satan comes immediately and takes away the word that was sown in their hearts. These likewise are the ones sown on stony ground who, when they hear the word, immediately receive it with gladness; and they have no root in themselves, and so endure only for a time. Afterward, when tribulation or persecution arises for the word's sake, immediately they stumble. Now these are the ones sown among thorns; they are the ones who hear the word, and the cares of this world, the deceitfulness of riches, and the desires for other things entering in choke the word, and it becomes unfruitful. But these are the ones sown on good ground, those who hear the word, accept it, and bear fruit: some thirtyfold, some sixty, and some a hundred.
(Mark 4:14–20)

But Martha was distracted with much serving, and she approached [Jesus] and said, "Lord, do You not care that my sister has left me to serve alone? Therefore tell her to help me." And Jesus answered and said to her, "Martha, Martha, you are worried and troubled about many things. But one thing is needed, and Mary has chosen that good part, which will not be taken away from her." (Luke 10:40–42)

The Works and Lusts of the Flesh

Now the works of the flesh are evident, which are: adultery, fornication, uncleanness, lewdness, idolatry, sorcery, hatred, contentions, jealousies, outbursts of wrath, selfish ambitions, dissensions, heresies, envy, murders, drunkenness, revelries, and the like; of which I tell you beforehand, just as I also told you in time past, that those who practice such things will not inherit the kingdom of God. (Galatians 5:19–21)

Do not love the world or the things in the world. If anyone loves the world, the love of the Father is not in him. For all that is in the world—the lust of the flesh, the lust of the eyes, and the pride of life—is not of the Father but is of the world. And the world is passing away, and the lust of it; but he who does the will of God abides forever. (1 John 2:15–17)

Do not be deceived, God is not mocked; for whatever a man sows, that he will also reap. For he who sows to his flesh will of the flesh reap corruption, but he who sows to the Spirit will of the Spirit reap everlasting life. (Galatians 6:7–8)

Come now, you who say, "Today or tomorrow we will go to such and such a city, spend a year there, buy and sell, and make a profit"; whereas you do not know what will happen tomorrow. For what is your life? It is even a vapor that appears for a little time and then vanishes away. Instead you ought to say, "If the Lord wills, we shall live and do this or that." But now you boast in your arrogance. All such boasting is evil. (James 4:13–16)

Now godliness with contentment is great gain. For we brought nothing into this world, and it is certain we can carry nothing out. And having food and clothing, with these we shall be content. But those who desire to be rich fall into temptation and a snare, and into many foolish and harmful lusts which drown men in destruction and perdition. For the love of money is a root of all kinds of evil, for which some have strayed from the faith in their greediness, and pierced themselves through with many sorrows. (1 Timothy 6:6–10)

Select Scriptures on the Keys and Gifts of God

Seeking the Kingdom

But seek the kingdom of God, and all these things shall be added to you. Do not fear, little flock, for it is your Father's good pleasure to give you the kingdom. Sell what you have and give alms; provide yourselves money bags which do not grow old, a treasure in the heavens that does not fail, where no thief approaches nor moth destroys. For where your treasure is, there your heart will be also. (Luke 12:31–34)

Binding and Loosing

Upon this rock I will build my church; and the gates of hell shall not prevail against it. And I will give unto thee the keys of the kingdom of heaven: and whatsoever thou shalt bind on earth shall be bound in heaven: and whatsoever thou shalt loose on earth shall be loosed in heaven.   (Matthew 16:18–19 KJV)

Assuredly, I say to you, whatever you bind on earth will be bound in heaven, and whatever you loose on earth will be loosed in heaven. Again I say to you that if two of you agree on earth concerning anything that they ask, it will be done for them by My Father in heaven. For where two or three are gathered together in My name, I am there in the midst of them.   (Matthew 18:18–20)

Jesus' Authority

The Spirit of the LORD is upon Me, because He has anointed Me to preach the gospel to the poor; He has sent Me to heal the brokenhearted, to proclaim liberty to the captives and recovery of sight to the blind, to set at liberty those who are oppressed.   (Luke 4:18)

God anointed Jesus of Nazareth with the Holy Spirit and with power, who went about doing good and healing all who were oppressed by the devil, for God was with Him.   (Acts 10:38)

And when He had called His twelve disciples to Him, He gave them power over unclean spirits, to cast them out, and to heal all kinds of sickness and all kinds of disease.   (Matthew 10:1)

Then [Jesus] went down to Capernaum, a city of Galilee, and was teaching them on the Sabbaths. And they were astonished at His teaching, for His word was

with authority. Now in the synagogue there was a man who had a spirit of an unclean demon. And he cried out with a loud voice, saying, "Let us alone! What have we to do with You, Jesus of Nazareth? Did You come to destroy us? I know who You are—the Holy One of God!" But Jesus rebuked him, saying, "Be quiet, and come out of him!" And when the demon had thrown him in their midst, it came out of him and did not hurt him. Then they were all amazed and spoke among themselves, saying, "What a word this is! For with authority and power He commands the unclean spirits, and they come out."
(Luke 4:31–36)

And Jesus came and spoke to [His disciples], saying, "All authority has been given to Me in heaven and on earth. Go therefore and make disciples of all the nations, baptizing them in the name of the Father and of the Son and of the Holy Spirit, teaching them to observe all things that I have commanded you; and lo, I am with you always, even to the end of the age."
(Matthew 28:18–20)

Having disarmed principalities and powers, [Jesus] made a public spectacle of them, triumphing over them in it. (Colossians 2:15)

God also has highly exalted [Jesus] and given Him the name which is above every name, that at the name of Jesus every knee should bow, of those in heaven, and of those on earth, and of those under the earth, and that every tongue should confess that Jesus Christ is Lord, to the glory of God the Father. (Philippians 2:9–11)

Most assuredly, I say to you, the hour is coming, and now is, when the dead will hear the voice of the Son of God; and those who hear will live. For as the Father has life in Himself, so He has granted the Son to have life in Himself, and has given Him authority to execute judgment also, because He is the Son of Man. Do not marvel at this; for the hour is coming in which all who are in the graves will hear His voice and come forth—those who have done good, to the resurrection of life, and those who have done evil, to the resurrection of condemnation.

(John 5:25–29)

The Name of Jesus

Then the seventy [disciples] returned with joy, saying, "Lord, even the demons are subject to us in Your name." And He said to them, "I saw Satan fall like lightning from heaven. Behold, I give you the authority to trample on serpents and scorpions, and over all the power of the enemy, and nothing shall by any means hurt you. Nevertheless do not rejoice in this, that the spirits are subject to you, but rather rejoice because your names are written in heaven." (Luke 10:17–20)

Most assuredly, I say to you, he who believes in Me, the works that I do he will do also; and greater works than these he will do, because I go to My Father. And whatever you ask in My name, that I will do, that the Father may be glorified in the Son. If you ask anything in My name, I will do it. (John 14:12–14)

And truly Jesus did many other signs in the presence of His disciples, which are not written in this book; but these are written that you may believe that Jesus is the Christ, the Son of God, and that believing you may have life in His name.   (John 20:30–31)

Then Peter, filled with the Holy Spirit, said to them, "Rulers of the people and elders of Israel: If we this day are judged for a good deed done to a helpless man, by what means he has been made well, let it be known to you all, and to all the people of Israel, that by the name of Jesus Christ of Nazareth, whom you crucified, whom God raised from the dead, by Him this man stands here before you whole. This is the 'stone which was rejected by you builders, which has become the chief cornerstone.' Nor is there salvation in any other, for there is no other name under heaven given among men by which we must be saved."   (Acts 4:8–12)

Now it happened, as we went to prayer, that a certain slave girl possessed with a spirit of divination met us, who brought her masters much profit by fortune-telling. This girl followed Paul and us, and cried out, saying, "These men are the servants of the Most High God, who proclaim to us the way of salvation." And this she did for many days. But Paul, greatly annoyed, turned and said to the spirit, "I command you in the name of Jesus Christ to come out of her." And he came out that very hour.   (Acts 16:16–18)

You did not choose Me, but I chose you and appointed you that you should go and bear fruit, and that your fruit should remain, that whatever you ask the Father in My name He may give you.   (John 15:16)

And these signs will follow those who believe: In My name they will cast out demons; they will speak with new tongues; they will take up serpents; and if they drink anything deadly, it will by no means hurt them; they will lay hands on the sick, and they will recover.
(Mark 16:17–18)

[Jesus'] name, through faith in His name, has made this man strong, whom you see and know. Yes, the faith which comes through Him has given him this perfect soundness in the presence of you all.   (Acts 3:16)

Obedience to God

Has the LORD as great delight in burnt offerings and sacrifices, as in obeying the voice of the LORD? Behold, to obey is better than sacrifice, and to heed than the fat of rams.   (1 Samuel 15:22)

Though [Jesus] was a Son, yet He learned obedience by the things which He suffered. And having been perfected, He became the author of eternal salvation to all who obey Him.   (Hebrews 5:8–9)

If you love Me, keep My commandments.
(John 14:15)

Through [Jesus] we have received grace and apostle-
ship for obedience to the faith among all nations for His
name.   (Romans 1:5)

Do you not know that to whom you present yourselves
slaves to obey, you are that one's slaves whom you obey,
whether of sin leading to death, or of obedience leading
to righteousness?   (Romans 6:16)

For the weapons of our warfare are not carnal but mighty
in God for pulling down strongholds, casting down arguments and every high thing that exalts itself against the
knowledge of God, bringing every thought into captivity
to the obedience of Christ, and being ready to punish all
disobedience when your obedience is fulfilled.
                                    (2 Corinthians 10:4–6)

Compassion

Then Jesus went about all the cities and villages, teaching
in their synagogues, preaching the gospel of the kingdom,
and healing every sickness and every disease among the
people. But when He saw the multitudes, He was moved
with compassion for them, because they were weary and
scattered, like sheep having no shepherd. Then He said
to His disciples, "The harvest truly is plentiful, but the
laborers are few."   (Matthew 9:35–37)

Repay no one evil for evil. Have regard for good things
in the sight of all men. If it is possible, as much as de-
pends on you, live peaceably with all men. Beloved, do
not avenge yourselves, but rather give place to wrath; for

it is written, "Vengeance is Mine, I will repay," says the Lord. Therefore "if your enemy is hungry, feed him; if he is thirsty, give him a drink; for in so doing you will heap coals of fire on his head." Do not be overcome by evil, but overcome evil with good. (Romans 12:17–21)

Brethren, if a man is overtaken in any trespass, you who are spiritual restore such a one in a spirit of gentleness, considering yourself lest you also be tempted. Bear one another's burdens, and so fulfill the law of Christ. (Galatians 6:1–2)

Finally, all of you be of one mind, having compassion for one another; love as brothers, be tenderhearted, be courteous; not returning evil for evil or reviling for reviling, but on the contrary blessing, knowing that you were called to this, that you may inherit a blessing. (1 Peter 3:8–9)

Love

"…And you shall love the LORD your God with all your heart, with all your soul, with all your mind, and with all your strength." This is the first commandment. And the second, like it, is this: "You shall love your neighbor as yourself." There is no other commandment greater than these. (Mark 12:30–31)

But I say to you, love your enemies, bless those who curse you, do good to those who hate you, and pray for those who spitefully use you and persecute you, that you may be sons of your Father in heaven; for He makes His sun rise on the evil and on the good, and sends rain on the just and on the unjust. For if you love those who love you, what reward have you? (Matthew 5:44–46)

Walk worthy of the calling with which you were called, with all lowliness and gentleness, with longsuffering, bearing with one another in love, endeavoring to keep the unity of the Spirit in the bond of peace.
(Ephesians 4:1–3)

Therefore be imitators of God as dear children. And walk in love, as Christ also has loved us and given Himself for us, an offering and a sacrifice to God for a sweet-smelling aroma. (Ephesians 5:1–2)

Let us consider how we may spur one another on toward love and good deeds. (Hebrews 10:24 NIV)

A Humble Spirit

Let nothing be done through selfish ambition or conceit, but in lowliness of mind let each esteem others better than himself. Let each of you look out not only for his own interests, but also for the interests of others.
(Philippians 2:3–4)

[Jesus] made Himself of no reputation, taking the form of a bondservant, and coming in the likeness of men. And being found in appearance as a man, He humbled Himself and became obedient to the point of death, even the death of the cross. Therefore God also has highly exalted Him…. (Philippians 2:7–9)

186 A Divine Revelation of Satan's Deceptions

Assuredly, I say to you, unless you are converted and become as little children, you will by no means enter the kingdom of heaven. Therefore whoever humbles himself as this little child is the greatest in the kingdom of heaven. Whoever receives one little child like this in My name receives Me. (Matthew 18:3–5)

Likewise you younger people, submit yourselves to your elders. Yes, all of you be submissive to one another, and be clothed with humility, for "God resists the proud, but gives grace to the humble." Humble yourselves under the mighty hand of God, that He may exalt you in due time, casting all your care upon Him, for He cares for you. (1 Peter 5:5–7)

But He gives more grace. Therefore He says: "God resists the proud, but gives grace to the humble." Therefore submit to God. Resist the devil and he will flee from you. Draw near to God and He will draw near to you. Cleanse your hands, you sinners; and purify your hearts, you double-minded. Lament and mourn and weep! Let your laughter be turned to mourning and your joy to gloom. Humble yourselves in the sight of the Lord, and He will lift you up. (James 4:6–10)

Spiritual Discernment

Beloved, do not believe every spirit, but test the spirits, whether they are of God; because many false prophets have gone out into the world. By this you know the Spirit of God: Every spirit that confesses that Jesus Christ has come in the flesh is of God, and every spirit that does

*not confess that Jesus Christ has come in the flesh is not
of God. And this is the spirit of the Antichrist, which
you have heard was coming, and is now already in the
world.* (1 John 4:1–3)

*If anyone says to you, "Look, here is the Christ!" or,
"Look, He is there!" do not believe it. For false christs
and false prophets will rise and show signs and wonders
to deceive, if possible, even the elect.* (Mark 13:21–22)

*And do not be conformed to this world, but be trans-
formed by the renewing of your mind, that you may
prove what is that good and acceptable and perfect will
of God.* (Romans 12:2)

*May [God the Father] give to you the spirit of wisdom
and revelation in the knowledge of Him, the eyes of your
understanding being enlightened; that you may know
what is the hope of His calling, what are the riches of the
glory of His inheritance in the saints, and what is the
exceeding greatness of His power toward us who believe,
according to the working of His mighty power.*
(Ephesians 1:17–19)

*And it shall come to pass in the last days, says God, that
I will pour out of My Spirit on all flesh; your sons and
your daughters shall prophesy, your young men shall see
visions, your old men shall dream dreams. And on My
menservants and on My maidservants I will pour out
My Spirit in those days; and they shall prophesy.*
(Acts 2:17–18)

*For everyone who partakes only of milk is unskilled in
the word of righteousness, for he is a babe. But solid food
belongs to those who are of full age, that is, those who by
reason of use have their senses exercised to discern both
good and evil.*   (Hebrews 5:13–14)

Praise

*The oil of joy for mourning, the garment of praise for the
spirit of heaviness.*   (Isaiah 61:3)

*Therefore by Him let us continually offer the sacrifice of
praise to God, that is, the fruit of our lips, giving thanks
to His name.*   (Hebrews 13:15)

*You are a chosen generation, a royal priesthood, a holy
nation, His own special people, that you may proclaim
the praises of Him who called you out of darkness into
His marvelous light.*   (1 Peter 2:9)

*But at midnight Paul and Silas were praying and singing
hymns to God, and the prisoners were listening to them.
Suddenly there was a great earthquake, so that the foun-
dations of the prison were shaken; and immediately all
the doors were opened and everyone's chains were loosed.
And the keeper of the prison, awaking from sleep and
seeing the prison doors open, supposing the prisoners
had fled, drew his sword and was about to kill himself.
But Paul called with a loud voice, saying, "Do yourself no
harm, for we are all here." Then he called for a light, ran
in, and fell down trembling before Paul and Silas. And
he brought them out and said, "Sirs, what must I do to be*

saved?" So they said, "Believe on the Lord Jesus Christ, and you will be saved, you and your household."

(Acts 16:25–31)

Whatever things are true, whatever things are noble, whatever things are just, whatever things are pure, whatever things are lovely, whatever things are of good report, if there is any virtue and if there is anything praiseworthy—meditate on these things. (Philippians 4:8)

Prayer

Therefore I say to you, whatever things you ask when you pray, believe that you receive them, and you will have them. And whenever you stand praying, if you have anything against anyone, forgive him, that your Father in heaven may also forgive you your trespasses.

(Mark 11:24–25)

Our Father in heaven, hallowed be Your name. Your kingdom come. Your will be done on earth as it is in heaven. Give us day by day our daily bread. And forgive us our sins, for we also forgive everyone who is indebted to us. And do not lead us into temptation, but deliver us from the evil one. (Luke 11:2–4)

Watch and pray, lest you enter into temptation. The spirit indeed is willing, but the flesh is weak.

(Mark 14:38)

When Jesus saw that the people came running together, He rebuked the unclean spirit, saying to it: "Deaf and dumb spirit, I command you, come out of him and enter him no more!" Then the spirit cried out, convulsed him greatly, and came out of him. And he became as one dead, so that many said, "He is dead." But Jesus took him by the hand and lifted him up, and he arose. And when He had come into the house, His disciples asked Him privately, "Why could we not cast it out?" So He said to them, "This kind can come out by nothing but prayer and fasting." (Mark 9:25–29)

Confess your trespasses to one another, and pray for one another, that you may be healed. The effective, fervent prayer of a righteous man avails much. (James 5:16)

Rejoice always, pray without ceasing, in everything give thanks; for this is the will of God in Christ Jesus for you. (1 Thessalonians 5:16–18)

The Spirit also helps in our weaknesses. For we do not know what we should pray for as we ought, but the Spirit Himself makes intercession for us with groanings which cannot be uttered. Now He who searches the hearts knows what the mind of the Spirit is, because He makes intercession for the saints according to the will of God. (Romans 8:26–27)

Praying always with all prayer and supplication in the Spirit, being watchful to this end with all perseverance and supplication for all the saints. (Ephesians 6:18)

The end of all things is at hand; therefore be serious and watchful in your prayers. (1 Peter 4:7)

Be anxious for nothing, but in everything by prayer and supplication, with thanksgiving, let your requests be made known to God; and the peace of God, which surpasses all understanding, will guard your hearts and minds through Christ Jesus.   (Philippians 4:6–7)

Therefore I exhort first of all that supplications, prayers, intercessions, and giving of thanks be made for all men, for kings and all who are in authority, that we may lead a quiet and peaceable life in all godliness and reverence.
(1 Timothy 2:1–2)

Men always ought to pray and not lose heart.
(Luke 18:1)

Righteousness

For I am the LORD your God. You shall therefore conse-crate yourselves, and you shall be holy; for I am holy.
(Leviticus 11:44)

For [God] made [Jesus] who knew no sin to be sin for us, that we might become the righteousness of God in Him.   (2 Corinthians 5:21)

For if by the one man's offense death reigned through the one, much more those who receive abundance of grace and of the gift of righteousness will reign in life through the One, Jesus Christ.   (Romans 5:17)

If anyone among you thinks he is religious, and does not bridle his tongue but deceives his own heart, this one's religion is useless. Pure and undefiled religion before God and the Father is this: to visit orphans and widows in their trouble, and to keep oneself unspotted from the world.   (James 1:26–27)

We know that whoever is born of God does not sin; but he who has been born of God keeps himself, and the wicked one does not touch him. We know that we are of God, and the whole world lies under the sway of the wicked one. And we know that the Son of God has come and has given us an understanding, that we may know Him who is true; and we are in Him who is true, in His Son Jesus Christ. This is the true God and eternal life.
                    (1 John 5:18–20)

Put off, concerning your former conduct, the old man which grows corrupt according to the deceitful lusts, and be renewed in the spirit of your mind, and…put on the new man which was created according to God, in true righteousness and holiness. Therefore, putting away lying, "Let each one of you speak truth with his neighbor," for we are members of one another. "Be angry, and do not sin": do not let the sun go down on your wrath, nor give place to the devil.   (Ephesians 4:22–27)

We have had human fathers who corrected us, and we paid them respect. Shall we not much more readily be in subjection to the Father of spirits and live? For they indeed for a few days chastened us as seemed best to them, but He for our profit, that we may be partakers of His holiness. Now no chastening seems to be joyful for the present, but painful; nevertheless, afterward it yields the

peaceable fruit of righteousness to those who have been
trained by it.   (Hebrews 12:9–11)

Do not let sin reign in your mortal body, that you should
obey it in its lusts. And do not present your members
as instruments of unrighteousness to sin, but present
yourselves to God as being alive from the dead, and your
members as instruments of righteousness to God. For sin
shall not have dominion over you, for you are not under
law but under grace.   (Romans 6:12–14)

The Word of God

This Book of the Law shall not depart from your mouth,
but you shall meditate in it day and night, that you may
observe to do according to all that is written in it. For
then you will make your way prosperous, and then you
will have good success.   (Joshua 1:8)

My people are destroyed for lack of knowledge.
                                                        (Hosea 4:6)

All Scripture is given by inspiration of God, and is prof-
itable for doctrine, for reproof, for correction, for instruc-
tion in righteousness, that the man of God may be com-
plete, thoroughly equipped for every good work.
                                        (2 Timothy 3:16–17)

Therefore lay aside all filthiness and overflow of wick-
edness, and receive with meekness the implanted word,
which is able to save your souls. But be doers of the word,
and not hearers only, deceiving yourselves. For if anyone

is a hearer of the word and not a doer, he is like a man observing his natural face in a mirror; for he observes himself, goes away, and immediately forgets what kind of man he was. But he who looks into the perfect law of liberty and continues in it, and is not a forgetful hearer but a doer of the work, this one will be blessed in what he does. (James 1:21–25)

For this reason we also thank God without ceasing, because when you received the word of God which you heard from us, you welcomed it not as the word of men, but as it is in truth, the word of God, which also effectively works in you who believe. (1 Thessalonians 2:13)

Faith

Now faith is the substance of things hoped for, the evidence of things not seen. (Hebrews 11:1)

For whatever is born of God overcomes the world. And this is the victory that has overcome the world—our faith. Who is he who overcomes the world, but he who believes that Jesus is the Son of God? (1 John 5:4–5)

Resist [your adversary, the devil], steadfast in the faith, knowing that the same sufferings are experienced by your brotherhood in the world. But may the God of all grace, who called us to His eternal glory by Christ Jesus, after you have suffered a while, perfect, establish, strengthen, and settle you. To Him be the glory and the dominion forever and ever. Amen. (1 Peter 5:9–11)

But without faith it is impossible to please [God], for he who comes to God must believe that He is, and that He is a rewarder of those who diligently seek Him.
(Hebrews 11:6)

Faith comes by hearing, and hearing by the word of God. (Romans 10:17)

For indeed the gospel was preached to us as well as to them; but the word which they heard did not profit them, not being mixed with faith in those who heard it.
(Hebrews 4:2)

The Fire of God

For [God] is like a refiner's fire and like launderer's soap. He will sit as a refiner and a purifier of silver; He will purify the sons of Levi, and purge them as gold and silver, that they may offer to the LORD an offering in righteousness. (Malachi 3:2–3)

"You shall trample the wicked, for they shall be ashes under the soles of your feet on the day that I do this," says the LORD of hosts. (Malachi 4:3)

[God] makes His angels spirits, His ministers a flame of fire. (Psalm 104:4)

John [the Baptist] answered, saying to all, "I indeed baptize you with water; but One mightier than I is coming, whose sandal strap I am not worthy to loose. He

[Jesus] will baptize you with the Holy Spirit and fire."

(Luke 3:16)

When the Day of Pentecost had fully come, they were all with one accord in one place. And suddenly there came a sound from heaven, as of a rushing mighty wind, and it filled the whole house where they were sitting. Then there appeared to them divided tongues, as of fire, and one sat upon each of them. And they were all filled with the Holy Spirit and began to speak with other tongues, as the Spirit gave them utterance.   (Acts 2:1–4)

Now when the thousand years have expired, Satan will be released from his prison and will go out to deceive the nations which are in the four corners of the earth, Gog and Magog, to gather them together to battle, whose number is as the sand of the sea. They went up on the breadth of the earth and surrounded the camp of the saints and the beloved city. And fire came down from God out of heaven and devoured them. The devil, who deceived them, was cast into the lake of fire and brimstone where the beast and the false prophet are. And they will be tormented day and night forever and ever.

(Revelation 20:7–10)

The Gifts of the Spirit

"Not by might nor by power, but by My Spirit," says the LORD *of hosts.*   (Zechariah 4:6)

And it shall come to pass afterward that I will pour out My Spirit on all flesh; your sons and your daughters shall prophesy, your old men shall dream dreams, your young men shall see visions. And also on My menservants and on My maidservants I will pour out My Spirit in those days.   (Joel 2:28–29)

Having then gifts differing according to the grace that is given to us, let us use them: if prophecy, let us prophesy in proportion to our faith; or ministry, let us use it in our ministering; he who teaches, in teaching; he who exhorts, in exhortation; he who gives, with liberality; he who leads, with diligence; he who shows mercy, with cheerfulness.   (Romans 12:6–8)

There are diversities of gifts, but the same Spirit. There are differences of ministries, but the same Lord. And there are diversities of activities, but it is the same God who works all in all. But the manifestation of the Spirit is given to each one for the profit of all: for to one is given the word of wisdom through the Spirit, to another the word of knowledge through the same Spirit, to another faith by the same Spirit, to another gifts of healings by the same Spirit, to another the working of miracles, to another prophecy, to another discerning of spirits, to another different kinds of tongues, to another the interpretation of tongues. But one and the same Spirit works all these things, distributing to each one individually as He wills.   (1 Corinthians 12:4–11)

And He Himself gave some to be apostles, some prophets, some evangelists, and some pastors and teachers, for the equipping of the saints for the work of ministry, for the edifying of the body of Christ.   (Ephesians 4:11–12)

Do not neglect the gift that is in you, which was given to you by prophecy with the laying on of the hands of the eldership. (1 Timothy 4:14)

Related Scriptures:

The Whole Armor of God

Finally, my brethren, be strong in the Lord and in the power of His might. Put on the whole armor of God, that you may be able to stand against the wiles of the devil. For we do not wrestle against flesh and blood, but against principalities, against powers, against the rulers of the darkness of this age, against spiritual hosts of wickedness in the heavenly places. Therefore take up the whole armor of God, that you may be able to withstand in the evil day, and having done all, to stand. Stand therefore, having girded your waist with truth, having put on the breastplate of righteousness, and having shod your feet with the preparation of the gospel of peace; above all, taking the shield of faith with which you will be able to quench all the fiery darts of the wicked one. And take the helmet of salvation, and the sword of the Spirit, which is the word of God; praying always with all prayer and supplication in the Spirit, being watchful to this end with all perseverance and supplication for all the saints. (Ephesians 6:10–18)

But let us who are of the day be sober, putting on the breastplate of faith and love, and as a helmet the hope of salvation. (1 Thessalonians 5:8)

The Fruit of the Spirit

But the fruit of the Spirit is love, joy, peace, longsuffering, kindness, goodness, faithfulness, gentleness, self-control. Against such there is no law.   (Galatians 5:22–23)

Do men gather grapes from thornbushes or figs from thistles? Even so, every good tree bears good fruit, but a bad tree bears bad fruit. A good tree cannot bear bad fruit, nor can a bad tree bear good fruit. Every tree that does not bear good fruit is cut down and thrown into the fire. Therefore by their fruits you will know them.
(Matthew 7:16–20)

For you were once darkness, but now you are light in the Lord. Walk as children of light (for the fruit of the Spirit is in all goodness, righteousness, and truth), finding out what is acceptable to the Lord. And have no fellowship with the unfruitful works of darkness, but rather expose them.   (Ephesians 5:8–11)

And this I pray, that your love may abound still more and more in knowledge and all discernment, that you may approve the things that are excellent, that you may be sincere and without offense till the day of Christ, being filled with the fruits of righteousness which are by Jesus Christ, to the glory and praise of God.   (Philippians 1:9–11)

The Blood of Jesus

Then [Jesus] took the cup, and gave thanks, and gave it to them, saying, "Drink from it, all of you. For this is My blood of the new covenant, which is shed for many for the remission of sins. (Matthew 26:27–28)

[Jesus] has delivered us from the power of darkness and conveyed us into the kingdom of the Son of His love, in whom we have redemption through His blood, the forgiveness of sins. (Colossians 1:13–14)

The blood of Christ, who through the eternal Spirit offered Himself without spot to God, [shall] cleanse your conscience from dead works to serve the living God. (Hebrews 9:14)

And they overcame him by the blood of the Lamb and by the word of their testimony, and they did not love their lives to the death. (Revelation 12:11)

Now I saw heaven opened, and behold, a white horse. And He who sat on him was called Faithful and True, and in righteousness He judges and makes war. His eyes were like a flame of fire, and on His head were many crowns. He had a name written that no one knew except Himself. He was clothed with a robe dipped in blood, and His name is called The Word of God. And the armies in heaven, clothed in fine linen, white and clean, followed Him on white horses. (Revelation 19:11–14)

Select Scriptures on Salvation and Jesus' Power to Keep Us in Him

Salvation

Multitudes, multitudes in the valley of decision! For the day of the LORD is near in the valley of decision.

(Joel 3:14)

Seek the LORD while He may be found, call upon Him while He is near. Let the wicked forsake his way, and the unrighteous man his thoughts; let him return to the LORD, and He will have mercy on him; and to our God, for He will abundantly pardon. (Isaiah 55:6–7)

God so loved the world that He gave His only begotten Son, that whoever believes in Him should not perish but have everlasting life. For God did not send His Son into the world to condemn the world, but that the world through Him might be saved. He who believes in Him is not condemned; but he who does not believe is condemned already, because he has not believed in the name of the only begotten Son of God. (John 3:16–18)

The Lord is…longsuffering toward us, not willing that any should perish but that all should come to repentance. (2 Peter 3:9)

If you confess with your mouth the Lord Jesus and believe in your heart that God has raised Him from the dead, you will be saved. For with the heart one believes unto righteousness, and with the mouth confession is made unto salvation. (Romans 10:9–10)

If we say that we have no sin, we deceive ourselves, and the truth is not in us. If we confess our sins, He is faithful and just to forgive us our sins and to cleanse us from all unrighteousness. (1 John 1:8–9)

And you He made alive, who were dead in trespasses and sins, in which you once walked according to the course of this world, according to the prince of the power of the air, the spirit who now works in the sons of disobedience, among whom also we all once conducted ourselves in the lusts of our flesh, fulfilling the desires of the flesh and of the mind, and were by nature children of wrath, just as the others. But God, who is rich in mercy, because of His great love with which He loved us, even when we were dead in trespasses, made us alive together with Christ (by grace you have been saved), and raised us up together, and made us sit together in the heavenly places in Christ Jesus, that in the ages to come He might show the exceeding riches of His grace in His kindness toward us in Christ Jesus. For by grace you have been saved through faith, and that not of yourselves; it is the gift of God, not of works, lest anyone should boast. For we are His workmanship, created in Christ Jesus for good works, which God prepared beforehand that we should walk in them. (Ephesians 2:1–10)

Jesus' Power to Keep Us in Him

Lo, I am with you always, even to the end of the age. (Matthew 28:20)

Peace I leave with you, My peace I give to you; not as the world gives do I give to you. Let not your heart be troubled, neither let it be afraid. (John 14:27)

My little children, these things I write to you, so that you may not sin. And if anyone sins, we have an Advocate with the Father, Jesus Christ the righteous. And He Himself is the propitiation for our sins, and not for ours only but also for the whole world. (1 John 2:1–2)

Now may the God of peace Himself sanctify you completely; and may your whole spirit, soul, and body be preserved blameless at the coming of our Lord Jesus Christ. He who calls you is faithful, who also will do it. (1 Thessalonians 5:23–24)

For in that He Himself has suffered, being tempted, He is able to aid those who are tempted. (Hebrews 2:18)

Who shall separate us from the love of Christ? Shall tribulation, or distress, or persecution, or famine, or nakedness, or peril, or sword? As it is written: "For Your sake we are killed all day long; we are accounted as sheep for the slaughter." Yet in all these things we are more than conquerors through Him who loved us. For I am persuaded that neither death nor life, nor angels nor principalities nor powers, nor things present nor things to come, nor height nor depth, nor any other created thing, shall be able to separate us from the love of God which is in Christ Jesus our Lord. (Romans 8:35–39)

The Lord is faithful, who will establish you and guard you from the evil one. (2 Thessalonians 3:3)

Seeing then that we have a great High Priest who has passed through the heavens, Jesus the Son of God, let us hold fast our confession. For we do not have a High Priest who cannot sympathize with our weaknesses, but was in all points tempted as we are, yet without sin. Let us therefore come boldly to the throne of grace, that we may obtain mercy and find grace to help in time of need. (Hebrew 4:14–16)

You are of God, little children, and have overcome them, because He who is in you is greater than he who is in the world. (1 John 4:4)

Now to Him who is able to keep you from stumbling, and to present you faultless before the presence of His glory with exceeding joy. (Jude 1:24)

About the Author

D r. Mary K. Baxter has been in full-time ministry for over thirty years, ever since she was taken by God into the dimensions and torments of hell, as well as the streets of heaven, for over forty nights in 1976. God commissioned Mary to record her experiences and tell others of the horrific depths, degrees, and torments of hell, as well as the wonderful destiny of heaven for the redeemed of Jesus Christ. There truly is a hell to shun and a heaven to gain!

Throughout her life, Mary has experienced many visions, dreams, and revelations of heaven, hell, and the spirit realm. She has been sent by God to minister in over 125 nations, and she has seen her books translated into more than twenty languages. Salvation springs forth as she walks in the miraculous power of God on her life. Signs and wonders follow her, and testimonies of God's saving grace abound in her ministry. She has a mother's heart to see all people come into the kingdom of God and become all that God has created them to be. She has birthed numerous other ministries and pours into the lives of others to see the kingdom of God expand into the emerging generations of the earth.

Mary was ordained as a minister in 1983 and received a Doctor of Ministry degree from Faith Bible College, an affiliate of Oral Roberts University. She continues to travel the world and minister in power. Mary is a best-selling author, and her previous books with Whitaker House include *A Divine Revelation of Hell*, *A Divine Revelation of Heaven*, *A Divine Revelation of the Spirit Realm*, *A Divine Revelation of Angels*, *A Divine Revelation of Spiritual Warfare*, *A Divine Revelation of Deliverance*, *A Divine Revelation of Healing*, *A Divine Revelation of Prayer*, and *The Power of the Blood*.

For speaking engagements, please contact:

Dr. Mary K. Baxter
Divine Revelation, Inc.
P.O. Box 121524
West Melbourne, FL 32912-1524

E-mail: marykbaxter1@yahoo.com
www.marykbaxterinc.com

Welcome to Our House!

We Have a Special Gift for You

It is our privilege and pleasure to share in your love of Christian books. We are committed to bringing you authors and books that feed, challenge, and enrich your faith.

To show our appreciation, we invite you to sign up to receive a specially selected **Reader Appreciation Gift**, with our compliments. Just go to the Web address at the bottom of this page.

God bless you as you seek a deeper walk with Him!

WE HAVE A GIFT FOR YOU. VISIT:

whpub.me/nonfictionthx

WHITAKER
HOUSE